The Zen Poetry of
DŌGEN

The Zen Poetry of
DŌGEN

*Verses from the
Mountain of Eternal Peace*

STEVEN HEINE

First published in 1997 by Tuttle Publishing, an imprint of Periplus Editions (HK) Ltd., with editorial offices at 153 Milk Street, Boston, Massachusetts 02109.

Copyright © 1997 Steven Heine

All rights reserved. No part of this publication may be reproduced or utilized in any form or by any means, electronic or mechanical, including photocopying, recording, or by any information storage and retrieval system, without prior written permission from Tuttle Publishing.

Library of Congress Catalog Card Number: 97–61734

DISTRIBUTED BY		
USA	JAPAN	SOUTHEAST ASIA
Charles E. Tuttle Co., Inc.	Tuttle Shokai Ltd.	Berkeley Books Pte. Ltd.
RR 1 Box 231-5	1-21-13, Seki	5 Little Road #08-01
North Clarendon, VT	Tama-ku, Kawasaki-shi	Singapore 536983
05759	Kanagawa-ken 214, Japan	Tel.: (65) 280-3320
Tel.: (802) 773-8930	Tel.: (044) 833-0225	Fax.: (65) 280-6290
Fax.: (802) 773-6993	Fax.: (044) 822-0413	

First edition
05 04 03 02 01   00 99 98 97   1 3 5 7 9 10 8 6 4 2

Design by Frances Kay
Cover design by Kathryn Sky-Peck

Printed in the United States of America

Contents

Preface vii

PART I THE ROLE OF POETRY IN DŌGEN'S APPROACH TO ZEN 1
Chapter One "Original Face": Dōgen and the Religio-Aesthetic
Tradition 1
Chapter Two Dewdrops on a Blade of Grass: Poetic Themes 35

PART II TRANSLATIONS OF THE JAPANESE AND CHINESE COLLECTIONS .. 89
Chapter Three A Small Boat Drifting: The Japanese Poetry
Collection 89
Chapter Four Treading Along in This Dreamlike World: Selections
from the Chinese Poetry Collection 121

APPENDIX A Selected Bibliography 147
APPENDIX B Chronology of Dōgen's Life 151
APPENDIX C Dōgen's Influence on Ryōkan 155

NOTES 161

Preface

THIS VOLUME contains a complete translation of Dōgen's collection of thirty-one-syllable Japanese poetry, or *waka,* along with a translation of a representative selection of his Chinese verse, or *kanshi.* Although Dōgen is generally considered to be more of a philosopher than a poet, his verse has great value for several reasons. First, the poems, most of which were composed on the mountain peak of Eiheiji Temple (the Temple of Eternal Peace, as pictured on the front cover), are beautiful, displaying Dōgen's remarkable facility with language. Second, the Japanese and Chinese collections illuminate key aspects of his life and thought not revealed in his prose writings, including his trips to China and Kamakura, his feelings about Kyoto while living in Eiheiji in the northern provinces, and his feelings about death. In addition, Dōgen's poetry, which was highlighted in Kawabata Yasunari's Nobel Prize acceptance speech of 1968, is important for understanding the relation between religion and the arts in medieval Buddhism and Japanese culture.

The first two chapters provide an introduction to the role of poetry in Dōgen's theory and practice in connection with the literary tradition. They give a compact overview of his thought, encompassing philosophical and aesthetic dimensions. They also show that literature plays a crucial role for Dōgen, despite the fact that the strict Zen master is often known for his emphasis on zazen meditation and his criticism of idle secular pursuits. For Dōgen, as for so many Buddhists of his era, if art is properly understood, it does not interfere with the enlightenment experience but complements or enhances it. The translations of the Japanese and Chinese verses appear in Chapters Three and Four, respectively. They are based on a careful reading of the sources and an attempt to capture the flavor of the delightful puns, wordplay, and irony of the originals.

Research for the translations was conducted at Komazawa University in Tokyo. I thank especially Professors Kawamura Kōdō, Yoshizu Yoshihide, and Ishii Shūdō for their invaluable assistance in guiding me through the history of the texts and commentaries on this material.

PART I

THE ROLE OF POETRY IN DŌGEN'S APPROACH TO ZEN

CHAPTER ONE

"Original Face": Dōgen and the Religio-Aesthetic Tradition

Dōgen, the Writer

TO APPRECIATE the significance of poetry in the life and thought of Dōgen (1200–1253), one must first consider the role of this Zen master and founder of the Sōtō sect in Kamakura-era Japan as a philosopher and as a writer. Dōgen's philosophical writings have received high praise for their literary qualities, especially their eloquent poetic flavor. The Zen tradition in medieval China and Japan is especially well known for its ingenuous teachers who awakened their disciples through dynamic, spontaneous "encounter dialogues" that are recorded in kōan collections such as the *Mumonkan* (Gateless gate) and *Hekiganroku* (Blue cliff record). However, many Zen patriarchs used language to defeat language, or as a "poison to counteract poison," resulting in a realization beyond thought and scripture. Dōgen, on the other hand, employs a variety of verbal devices such as philosophical wordplay, paradox, and irony in order to stress that there is a fundamental identity of language and enlightenment, or a oneness of the sutras and personal attainment. Rather than emphasizing silence or the transcendence of speech, Dōgen proves himself in his main work, the *Shōbōgenzō,* to be a master of language. He exhibits remarkable skill in revealing how ordinary words harbor a deeper though generally hidden metaphysical meaning. Thus, according to Tanabe Hajime, one of the leading modern philosophers in Japan associated with the Kyoto School, "viewed from the philosophical standpoint, Dōgen's *Shōbōgenzō* is matchless in its command of Japanese language and logic with the power to realize the ineffable in and through speech and discussion."[1] Hee-Jin Kim, one of the first scholars to work on Dōgen studies in the West in the 1970s, argues that "Dōgen's originality lies in his radical transformation of language."[2]

One of the main examples of Dōgen's creativity is the philosophical pun he makes on the word *uji* (also pronounced *arutoki*), a word that in everyday conversation means "sometimes," but that is composed of two *kanji* (Chinese characters) for "being" *(u)* and "time" *(ji).* In the *Shōbōgenzō* "Uji" (Being-time) fascicle Dōgen uses *uji* to imply the principle of the paradoxical unity of "being-time." Being, or all beings in space, and time, or all moments of existence in the three tenses, are viewed not in opposition but as a synthetic wholeness in that "all beings are all times."[3] In the same fascicle Dōgen's writing displays the intimate connection between philosophical ideas and poetic expression in the following passage: "The arousing of aspiration [in different] minds at the selfsame time is the arousing [at different times] of the selfsame mind *(dōji ho(tsu)shin ari, dōshin ho(tsu)ji ari)."*[4] By reversing the order of the characters *ji* (time) and *shin* (mind) in the two clauses, Dōgen offers a concrete literary expression of the meaning of the interpenetration of temporality and consciousness, universality and particularity, and resolve and attainment.

Another instance is his rereading in the "Busshō" (Buddha-nature) fascicle of the Mahayana Buddhist saying "All beings have the Buddha-nature" as "whole-being-Buddha-nature" *(shitsu-u-busshō),* based on the twofold meaning of *u* as "to be" as well as "to have," in order to eliminate a sense that ultimate reality is an object possessed by individuals.⁵ Furthermore, Dōgen often reinterprets traditional kōans, such as the famous case of Chaochou answering *Wu* (Jap. *Mu;* lit. "no") to the question of whether a dog has Buddha-nature, so that they do not end in silence but the dialogue continues to explore diverse philosophical implications. In general, Dōgen stresses that language and symbols should be used positively and constructively as a revelation of the absolute. He contrasts his approach with what he considers the problematic Zen view that speech is an obstacle or barrier to realization that must be abandoned. "It is a pity," he writes, "that [the conventional Zen masters] do not know that thought is words and phrases, or that words and phrases release (or break through) thought."⁶

Dōgen's approach to language as a poetic means of expresssing the truth of the paradoxical universality of Buddhanature as a here-and-now temporal process at once epitomizes and forges a new path within the Zen philosophical tradition. This is especially interesting because, although poetic expression is a key to Dōgen's philosophy, there is another reason that his works have been seen as standing in contrast to the mainstream of Zen literature, which for the most part greatly values the composition of verse per se. Dōgen is often cited not for the writing of poetry but actually for the reverse: for a famous admonition in the *Shōbōgenzō zuimonki* collection of lectures against an indulgence in literary pursuits that distracts from a supreme, single-minded dedication to attaining the Buddhist Dharma. Known for an uncompromising commitment to just-sitting in *zazen* meditation *(shikan-taza),* he criticized the apparent corruption of religious practice by any interest in secular pursuits, including literature and aesthetics.

On the other hand, like nearly all medieval Zen masters, Dōgen was an accomplished poet who left behind two important collections of poetry: one in Japanese, and one in Chinese. The Japanese collection, consisting of sixty-three *waka* verses, was first published in the main biography of Dōgen, the *Kenzeiki* (1472), released over two hundred years after his death. It has traditionally been known as *Sanshōdōei* or *Verses on the Way from Sanshō Peak*. Sanshō was the original name for the location of Eiheiji Temple (literally, the Temple of Eternal Peace), the remote mountain monastery where Dōgen, in retreat from the capital in Kyoto, spent the last ten years of his life. The waka, a style of verse composed for medieval Japanese imperial collections though used far less frequently by Zen masters, contains five lines with thirty-one syllables following a 5-7-5-7-7 scheme. It features numerous techniques for employing puns, homophones, wordplay, and other verbal associations to explore lyrical and natural themes. These devices seem to have been a major influence on Dōgen's view of language. Dōgen's Chinese poetry collection, or *kanshi*, contained as part of the ten-volume *Eihei kōroku* recorded-sayings text, is considerably longer and more complex than the waka collection. The main parts consist of about a hundred and fifty verses on lyrical themes and ninety verses commenting on kōan cases, or dialogues between Zen masters and disciples, in the last two volumes of the *Eihei kōroku*, usually in a verse style of four lines with seven characters each. In addition to these two main groups of Chinese poetry, there are nearly one hundred kanshi that are part of the sermons and lectures contained in the first eight volumes of the *Eihei kōroku*. The kanshi-style poems, perfected by Zen masters in the school of "Five Mountains literature" *(Gozan bungaku)* in Japan, are written entirely with Chinese characters *(kanji)*, though their rhyme schemes are generally based on Japanese pronunciation rather than Chinese tones.[7]

Japanese waka and Chinese kanshi adhere to very different conventions involving syntax and diction, but both forms use natural imagery, especially relating to the changing of the seasons, and both allow the author room to explore a range of emotions from the personal and introspective to a more detached and aloof standpoint. Nearly all the waka and the great majority of the kanshi were composed at the Mountain of Eternal Peace (Eiheiji). They celebrate the natural splendor of the location, in Echizen province, a travel site often depicted in Japanese Court poetry, while also expressing a sense of longing to return to the capital, which is a source of attraction because of both its refined culture and its natural beauty. The poetry collections are extremely valuable for demonstrating the development of Dōgen's philosophical interests in language and impermanence from the period of his four-year journey to China (1223–1227), where he attained enlightenment under the guidance of Master Ju-ching (Jap. Nyojō), through his career in Japan, where he established the first large Zen monastic institution. The verses complement and enhance our understanding of the *Shōbōgenzō* and other prose works. The kanshi collection reveals Dōgen eager to emulate the model of the great masters in Sung-era China who were influenced by the Confucian intellectual elite, and the Japanese collection represents the initial composition of waka by a master of the newly emerging Zen sect influenced by Court poetry. Furthermore, Dōgen's effort to write verse in the indigenous language dovetails with the fact that the *Shōbōgenzō*, which was the first major Buddhist work composed in Japanese, borrows much of its rhetorical flavor and spiritual insights from techniques commonly used in the aesthetic traditions of medieval Japan. The waka collection highlights Dōgen's affinity with leading figures of the period who combined literary pursuits with Buddhist contemplation, such as the poets Saigyō and Teika and the critics Chōmei and Kenkō, as well as later authors who cited his influence on their spiritual approach to literature; these include the Noh playwright and theorist Zeami and Edo-era poets Ryōkan and Bashō.[8] For example, Ryōkan, a practitioner of Sōtō Zen who was known ironically as "Great Fool" (Daigu) for his creative genius, wrote over a dozen waka as variations on Dōgen's originals, and he also composed numerous Chinese poems as commentaries on passages and themes from the *Shōbōgenzō* and *Eihei kōroku* (see Appendix C for a fuller discussion of Ryōkan's role). Also Bashō was inspired by his visit to the mountain hermitage of Eiheiji, as noted in his poetic diary, *Oku no hosomichi*.

Dōgen's facility with language reflects an indebtedness to the major literary methods and conceits of the Japanese poetic tradition, such as the use of pivot-words *(kakekotoba)*, relational words *(engo)*, and allusive variation *(honkadori)*. These waka techniques, which sometimes seem to go against the ordinary grammatical structure of language, are "a direct means of achieving a polyphonic plenitude of meanings, images and ideas."⁹ The use of these techniques, together with the rewriting of earlier poems, brings out the multiple and intertwining connotations of conventional images through complex wordplay. In addition, the "conciseness and toughness" of expression that commentators often note in Dōgen's language may parallel the poetic ideal of using "sparse words" *(kotoba tarazu)* or "words that are too few" to convey an "overflow of feeling" *(yojō)*—that is, a minimum of language to suggest a multitude of implications.¹⁰ Also Dōgen's view of the passage of time seems very much influenced by an aesthetic attunement to nature as the main model for understanding impermanent reality. His intensely personal response to dying and transiency, rooted in the loss of his parents when he was a child, culminates in the doctrine of the impermanence of Buddha-nature *(mujō-busshō)*, or of ultimate reality being equated with all natural phenomena rotating cyclically through the four seasons.

Furthermore, both poetry collections are important for understanding Dōgen's biography, particularly his attitudes at crucial turning points that are not revealed by other, more didactic prose writings. For several periods in Dōgen's life, the poetry is actually the only extant material with which we can interpret what happened or how he felt about his life. For example, about fifty kanshi he composed in China are the only existing writings from that time, and twelve waka and one kanshi are the only works from Dōgen's eight-month trip (1247–1248) to preach before the shogun, Hōjō Tokiyori, in what was then a Rinzai sect stronghold in the temporary capital in Kamakura. In addition, he composed several verses about his enlightenment experience and his impending death—conventional themes for Zen poets—as well as writings about his sense of longing to return to Kyoto during his stay in Eiheiji.

Chapter One 7

This book provides a translation of the entire waka collection as well as a representative selection of different styles of Dōgen's kanshi poems. Preceding the translations is a discussion of the role of poetry and aesthetics in Dōgen's life and thought. The discussion that follows explores the fundamental creative tension or constructive ambivalence in Dōgen's verse concerning the relation between religion and art, or Buddhist meditation and aesthetic reflection, and shows that this tension or ambivalence connected Dōgen to the religio-aesthetic or contemplative tradition in Japan. Chapter Two explores systematically the role of lyrical, didactic, and personal themes running through the two collections. The poems are cited by number according to the translations that appear in Chapters Three and Four; a *J* (for example, #1-J) indicates the Japanese collection, and a *C* (#1-C) indicates the Chinese collection.

Kawabata's Comments on the Waka "Original Face"

Primarily because of the *Shōbōgenzō zuimonki* admonition against indulging in literary pursuits, Dōgen's poetry received relatively little attention from traditional commentators, except for biographers who cite the verse as evidence of historical events. The *Shōbōgenzō,* considered the premier philosophical work in Japanese history, is the subject of numerous commentaries and translations, but Dōgen's verse has been seen as far less important than that of his contemporaries who wrote poems. His poems were not included in the major poetry collections of their period, and even within the Sōtō sect there were only a small handful of commentaries on the waka collection from the Tokugawa era. But the inattention to and neglect of Dōgen's poetry, especially of his Japanese waka, changed dramatically three decades ago. In 1968 Kawabata Yasunari, the first Japanese author to win the Nobel Prize for literature, opened his acceptance speech in Stockholm rather surprisingly, much to the wonder of members of the Zen community, by citing a waka composed by Dōgen. In the speech, entitled "Japan, the Beautiful, and Myself" *(Utsukushii Nihon no watakushi),* Kawabata commented on the profound influence of different aspects of Zen aesthetics on his writing, beginning with Dōgen's verse. In Edward Seidensticker's translation of Kawabata's speech, the waka (#14-J in this book) reads:[11]

> *Haru wa hana*   In the spring, cherry blossoms,
> *Natsu hototogisu*   In the summer the cuckoo,
> *Aki wa tsuki*   In autumn the moon, and in
> *Fuyu yuki kiede*   winter the snow, clear, cold.
> *Suzushi kari keri.*

This poem is notable, according to Kawabata, because "by a spontaneous though deliberate stringing together of conventional images and words, it transmits the very essence of Japan."[12] Kawabata refers to "conventional images and words" in Dōgen's verse in a special sense, expressing a simple connecting of seasonal imagery typical of medieval poetry in evoking the ephemeral yet cyclical quality of the beauty of nature, which springs directly from the deepest sources of the Japanese poetic tradition. The general topic of Zen and literature is by no means unique. Indeed, Kawabata's comments have been criticized for contributing to a stereotypical, uncritical romanticization and idealization of traditional Japan.[13] But Kawabata's citation of Dōgen's waka was at the time striking and unusual because Dōgen probably did not consider the composition of poetry an important endeavor, and in a cultural tradition marked by a profound convergence of religion and aesthetics, Dōgen seems to be distinctive for his strong criticism of literature.

Many commentators have analyzed the fundamental connection between religion and art throughout much of the history of thought and culture in Japan. The modern Indian poet Rabindranath Tagore has referred to aesthetics as Japan's "unique Dharma."[14] Kishimoto Hideo remarks, "In their achievements, religious values and aesthetic values are not two different things.

figure 1. *Four Seasons at Eiheiji*

This painting on a single sheet of handmade Japanese paper offers a panoramic view of Eiheiji and suggests the four seasons—winter at the top, spring to the left, fall to the right, and summer at the bottom.

Ultimately, they are one for the Japanese."[15] Also Richard Pilgrim categorizes the artistic way—in the sense that literature and poetry (along with the fine arts and other art forms) are pursued as a "way" (*dō* or *michi*, Chin. *tao*) of subjective, personal spiritual attainment—in terms of the pervasive "religio-aesthetic" tradition of Japan. According to Pilgrim, this tradition is one "in which artistic form and aesthetic sensibility become synonomous with religious form and religious (or spiritual) sensibility."[16]

Yet Dōgen apparently draws a clear and consistent line between religion and art, warning his disciples against the pursuit of "style and rhetoric," which may distract from or impede their spiritual development. "Impermanence moves swiftly," he says in *Shōbōgenzō zuimonki*. "The meaning of life and death is the great problem. In this short life, if you want to practice and study, you must follow the Buddha Way and study the Buddha Dharma. The composition of literature, Chinese poetry and Japanese verse is worthless, and it must be renounced."[17] He adds in another passage, "Zen monks are fond of literature these days, finding it an aid to writing verses and tracts. This is a mistake. . . . Yet no matter how elegant their prose or how exquisite their poetry might be, they are merely toying with words and cannot gain the truth."[18] This critique comes from a Zen master celebrated for continually editing and reediting his elegant *Shōbōgenzō* prose throughout his career.

Furthermore, the distinction indicated by Dōgen between "art for art's sake" and the search for truth, or between an idle indulgence in literature and an exclusive determination to fulfill the religious quest, seems to have been played out in his own life. His biography, according to traditional sources (which modern research has shown to be marred from a historiographical standpoint by considerable hagiographical excess), gives prominence to the renunciation and departure from the elite, aesthete world of the Kyoto Court aristocracy on three main occasions in his life.[19] But it is just these events, or at least Dōgen's reactions to them, that are often primarily recorded not in his prose writings but in his poetry. First, Dōgen's decision to become a monk at the age of thirteen was an abandonment of the Court career awaiting him. Dōgen's initial affiliation with the Court, the sources indicate, was owing to his aristocratic background as the son and then the stepson of prominent nobles who were also famous poets and contributors to the leading imperial anthology of the era, the *Shinkokinshū*. Orphaned at age seven, Dōgen was overwhelmed by grief and a sense of transiency as he saw the smoke rising from the incense burned at his mother's funeral. He continued to feel a keen sense of the sorrow of impermanence and a profound longing for release from suffering, which led him to join the monkhood. At twenty-four, Dōgen left the dominant Tendai Buddhist as well as the newly formed Zen monasteries in the area of Kyoto and Mt. Hiei to seek the authentic Dharma in Sung China because he considered the Japanese Buddhist institutions to be corrupt and secularized. Dōgen had a "great doubt" about the need for sustained practice. If, as the established sects claimed, all things originally were of the Buddha-nature, the need to train diligently to attain enlightenment would seem to be vitiated.

Finally, at age forty-four, sixteen years after returning to Japan from China, where he resolved the doubt while training with Ju-ching, Dōgen again renounced the secularized and politicized atmosphere of Kyoto Buddhism. He left the capital to establish a strictly disciplined monastic order, which eventually became the Sōtō sect. Dōgen settled in Eiheiji Temple, situated in the relatively remote mountains of Echizen Province (present-day Fukui prefecture, near Kawabata's "snow country"), a place eloquently described in many of his poems. Eiheiji is in close proximity to Mt. Hakusan, a snow-covered peak that was long one of the primary sacred mountains in Japan and a practice site for mountain ascetics known as *yamabushi*. It also inspired several of Dōgen's poems and now serves as a location for pilgrimages and

figure 2. *Mt. Hakusan*

A view of the snow-covered peak of Mt. Hakusan, the central sacred mountain of the area in Echizen Province (present-day Fukui), where Dōgen established Eiheiji Temple in the 1240s. Hakusan was a site of great beauty in Japanese poetry and has also been a prime location for mountain ascetics *(yamabushi)* as well as a retreat area for Sōtō monks in training.

summer retreats for Sōtō monks in training. The following waka (#39-J) conveys the beauty of this landscape ironically by portraying the monochromatic image of a cold and snowy mountain:

Waga iho wa	The white mountain of Echizen
Koshi no shirayama	My winter retreat:
Fuyugomori	A blanket of clouds
Kōri mo yuki mo	Covering the frosted peaks
Kumo kakari keri.	And snowy slopes.

The successive shades and textures of wintry whiteness are accentuated by the wordplay on *shirayama* (lit. "white mountain," another pronunciation of Mt. Hakusan). Perhaps the Buddhist doctrine of nondifferentiation allowing infinite varieties of distinction is suggested here, as in a Zen saying cited by Zeami that a white heron reflected by the moonlight sits by a silver vase.

Dōgen apparently enjoyed the fact that Eiheiji, supported by a wealthy patron, Hatano Yoshishige, was independent of the sectarian conflicts and secular distractions of Kyoto. Although a number of Dōgen's disciples hailed from the region of Echizen, many others training under his supervision needed to make a taxing journey, testing their commitment. This last move from Kyoto seems to represent the culmination of Dōgen's disdain for the Court and its pervasive influence on the Buddhist institutions, a feeling also held by other leading Kamakura-era reformers such as Hōnen (founder of the Pure Land sect), Shinran (founder of the True Pure Land sect), and Nichiren (founder of the Nichiren sect). Dōgen returned to Kyoto one time for medical care shortly before his death, a journey recorded only in his waka, which express his mixed emotions for the capital. The two poems on Dōgen's final journey are among the most moving and memorable in the collection. Poem #2-J is based on an ambiguous reference to the viewing of the harvest moon, a traditional occasion for contemplation and the composition of poetry:

Mata minto	Just when my longing to see

Omoishi toki no	The moon over Kyoto
Aki dani mo	One last time grows deepest,
Koyoi no tsuki ni	The image I behold this autumn
	night
Nerare yawa suru.	Leaves me sleepless for its beauty.

The word *moon* (*tsuki*) appears one time in the original, so that the phrase *mata minto* (lit. "seeing again") makes it unclear to which moon Dōgen's longing refers: is it the Kyoto moon he has missed for ten years, as suggested by the translation, or the harvest moon of the following year, which he realizes he may not live to see? In either case, there is a haunting sense of melancholy concerning the full moon, which represents an irresistible attraction to natural beauty. Dōgen's anxiety and longing converge and collapse at the sudden understanding that the moon he hopes to see at some time in the future is none other than the one he currently beholds. The irony cannot be missed that Dōgen chides himself for almost neglecting the message so fundamental to his Zen teaching: that the present moment should be experienced as it is in its pure, unadorned form without recourse to the self-created distractions of expectation and regret. The poem concludes with a sense of thankfulness and wonderment based on a personal experience that clarifies the nature of time.

Therefore, despite some textual and biographical factors that tend to argue against Dōgen's having held poetry in high regard, his waka lyrically convey a human response to transiency, as reflected in the turning of the seasons, that points to the non-substantive or impermanent ground of existence. The poem Kawabata cites is titled "Original Face" (*honrai no memmoku;* Seidensticker's rendering is "Innate Spirit"), a traditional Zen motto for primordial human nature attributed to sixth patriarch Hui-neng in an anecdote cited in the *Mumonkan* kōan collection case 23. It also recalls the verse comment on case 19 ("Ordinary mind is Tao") of the *Mumonkan:*[20]

In spring hundreds of flowers, in autumn the clear moon,

In summer a cool breeze, and in winter the white snow,
If your mind is free of vanity, then every season is fine.

For Kawabata, Dōgen's verse is noteworthy as art, and not merely for its instructive meaning or for the philosophical implications couched in poetic language. There may be other poems in Dōgen's collections that are less significant from an aesthetic standpoint and convey a basically moral, didactic, or autobiographical message.

But the implications of the style and content of "Original Face" are not Buddhist in contrast to aesthetic. Rather the poem divulges the "essence of Japan." It is a lyric and symbolic disclosure of the religio-aesthetic understanding of human existence in relation to time, nature, the four seasons, and ultimate reality. It recalls Kūkai's famous *i ro ha* "alphabet" verse, which illustrates the integration of Buddhist and Japanese elements in expressing the relation between impermanence, symbolized by "falling blossoms," and subjective realization, represented by the image of "crossing deep mountain paths" to awaken from the "dream" of "illusory activities." We are also reminded of Kenkō's view of seasonal transition in *Tsurezuregusa:* "It is not that when spring draws to a close it becomes summer, or that when summer ends the autumn comes: spring itself urges the summer to show itself . . . the leaves fall because the budding from underneath is too powerful to resist."[21] "Original Face" thus fulfills the fact that "[i]t is characteristic of the Japanese absorption with nature that their *momento mori* should be . . . live, poignant images like the scattering of blossoms or the yellowing of autumn leaves, which served to remind them that all beautiful things must soon pass away."[22] Following from this, it appears that Dōgen's use of Japanese literary techniques in writing the *Shōbōgenzō* was not for the sake of popularizing Buddhism, as in the case of Mūjū's *Shasekishū* collection of pious tales about common folk, or for nationalistic aspirations as with the works of eighteenth-century National Learning scholars *(Kokugakusha).* Rather, as Katō Shūichi points out, "The author's purpose in writing [in Japanese] was not for the benefit of his readers but for the sake of the Way, and the essence of prose to Dōgen was to write down his argument, just as he thought it . . . [demonstrating] a remarkable ability for swiftly changing from the abstract to the concrete and back again to the abstract in his thinking."[23]

Yet these comments concerning the role of language as the distinctively Japanese element in Dōgen's thought need clarification. Japanese is in no way better suited to articulating the Buddhist Dharma than is Chinese. Nor is Dōgen necessarily more influenced by his native language than by his acquired one. In some ways it is the more direct impact of kanshi poetry on Dōgen that can be established. Many Chinese Zen masters are applauded for their creativity in manipulating language through wordplay, paradoxes, and other techniques that are used to extract the philosophical significance from everyday speech, though they tend to reach a different conclusion about the meaning of discourse than Dōgen does. The *Shōbōgenzō*, which consists mainly of Japanese commentaries on passages from sutras and Zen sayings written in Chinese, depends on an understanding of the implications of the source language. In addition, many of Dōgen's writings are in Chinese, such as the sermons in the *Eihei kōroku*, the kōan cases in the *Shōbōgenzō sanbyakusoku*, and the instructions on meditation in *Fukanzazengi*. Dōgen's collection of Chinese poems is much larger than his waka collection. His literary sensibility and skill are based in large part on the influence of the Chinese verse of Ju-ching and a predecessor of his teacher, Hung-chih (Jap. Wanshi), who is renowned for both his Zen poetry and the kōan collection, the *Shōyōroku* (Record of serenity). Dōgen refers to both Ju-ching and Hung-chih by the affectionate term "old master" *(kobutsu)*. He also greatly admired the poetic character of the *Hekiganroku*, which he was said to have copied in a single night just before returning from China.[24] The following kanshi, #8-C, demonstrates Dōgen's use of Chinese to describe the turning of the seasons by focusing on the image of plum blossoms, which have a fragrance that symbolizes the emergence of spring at the very end of winter:

> *Outside my window, plum blossoms,*
> *Just on the verge of unfurling, contain the spring;*
> *The clear moon is held in the cuplike petals*
> *Of the beautiful flower I pick, and twirl.*

The Relation Between Religion and Art

The opposition between religion and art that was played out in Dōgen's religious life and his poetic work involves an interplay between the relative and the absolute, attachment and realization, and objectivity and subjectivity. Dōgen's approach is based on his awakening experience of "casting off body-mind" *(shinjin datsuraku),* or his liberation from all volitional attachments and mental constructions concerning objectifiable forms. His writing exemplifies the "compassionate words" expressing the truth of Buddhist Dharma, the sole aim of which is to convey one's own realization in order to assist others on their path to the attainment of enlightenment. Dōgen criticizes literature for its interest in the external world of relative forms, which the writer objectifies in trying to grasp an inauthentic subjective or emotional reaction to change and instability. Poetry, as an example of "dramatic phrases and flowery words" *(kyōgen-kigo),* attempts eloquently but in the end miguidedly, from this perspective, to capture feelings of longing, sorrow, loss, expectation, or uncertainty that reflect a partial awareness of evanescence. Dōgen suggests that poetry may fail to express an authentic or detached and impersonal realization of the absolute truth of impermanent, nonsubstantive existence. Thus literature deals with an emotional attachment to form and words, while Buddhist enlightenment concentrates on cultivating an attitude of impartiality toward reality beyond the opposites of life and death, love and hate, and speech and silence.

Where does Dōgen really stand on the issue of religion and aesthetics? Should we disregard his admonitions in *Shōbōgenzō zuimonki,* or should we view them as an inconsistency? According

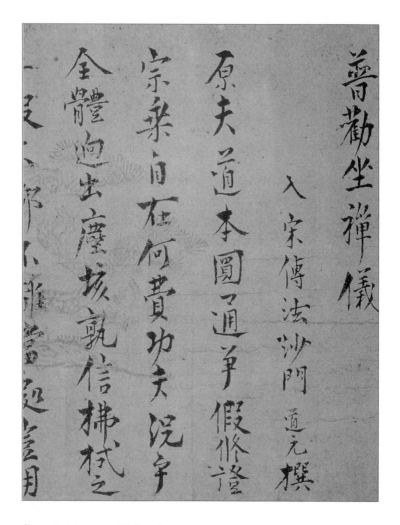

figure 3. *Fukanzazengi Calligraphy*

The opening passage in the calligraphy by Dōgen's own hand of his meditation manual, the *Fukanzazengi*. The formal style of writing on special paper conveys Dōgen's aristocratic upbringing and is often recognized as one of the main examples of calligraphy in a culture that highly prizes this art form.

to one commentator, Dōgen's approach may be categorized as a "literary critique of literature" (or a "literature which negates literature," *bungei futei no bungei*).[25] Others point out that Dōgen's conception of what his writing means does not necessarily prohibit the reader from adapting an interpretation to which he himself would probably say, "That should not be discussed!"[26] The need for an audience-specific interpretation is noted by Masunaga Reihō, a modern Sōtō scholar who completed the first translation into English of a Dōgen text, the *Shōbōgenzō zuimonki*: "At times the followers are exhorted to follow the conduct of their predecessors in Zen; at times they are cautioned to ignore them. Such inconsistencies develop in part, perhaps, from the different levels from which Dōgen talks; at times he is the mentor to virtual beginners, and his approach is the simple one that explains the requisites for study."[27] An example illustrating Masunaga's contention occurs when Dōgen encourages individuality and independence by advising monks against reading Zen recorded sayings (*goroku*) in the same passage in which he dismisses literature. In other passages, however, Dōgen stresses that monks should "disregard their own minds in following the words and actions of the Buddhas and Patriarchs, whether they seem good or bad." Dōgen's aim is neither to confuse nor to attack blindly. Rather, he criticizes certain misunderstandings and abuses of religious approaches by those who are unable to apply them appropriately to Zen realization. It is also important to note that aside from the passages cited, Dōgen does not specifically reject poetry or literature in his philosophical writings, particularly the *Shōbōgenzō*. In fact, interpretations of Chinese Zen poems fill his master work. The "Zazenshin" (Prescription for zazen) fascicle, for instance, consists of his interpretation and rewriting of Hung-chih's verse by that title (see #48-C). Another indication of his aesthetic side is that Dōgen, with his aristocratic background and education, was an outstanding calligrapher whose formal script is often cited in studies of medieval art.

Furthermore, Dōgen's interpretive stance on Zen sayings, poems, and Mahayana scriptures depends upon alchemical wordplay reflecting aesthetic influence. In seeking to draw out multiple shades and nuances embedded though unrecognized in the source material, he demonstrates the inherent unity of language and reality. Although he generally stresses reason (*dōri*) as the basis of Dōgen's approach to language, the scholar Hee-Jin Kim also argues that "for all his admonitions against play with words, he was deeply poetic and, as a medieval Japanese, he could not have been otherwise. To Dōgen, to philosophize was not only to think but also to feel, not only to rationalize but also to poeticize."[28] The value of Dōgen's affirmation of aesthetic awareness has been recognized by his Sōtō interpreter Suzuki Shōsan. Suzuki records being asked by a disciple if the composing of waka #2-J, which expresses Dōgen's longing for the Kyoto moon, was not incompatible with Dōgen's otherwise uncompromising insistence on emotional detachment. Suzuki responds, "You are wrong. Dōgen diverted himself with writing [waka].... We should sing of the moons and flowers from the bottom of our heart. You seem to think it will do only if you say, 'No delusion should be harbored; everything should be relinquished.'"[29] According to Suzuki, for Dōgen there is a sense of being unable to resist the aesthetic feelings generated by natural forms, from which one "cannot help" but be drawn into an emotional response. In addition, Dōgen frequently mentions in *Shōbōgenzō zuimonki* and other writings that his deeply personal experience of transiency through the early loss of his parents was a crucial emotional factor in the awakening of his resolve (*hosshin*) for enlightenment. Although enlightenment lies beyond emotionalism, the inspiration to seek attainment is based largely on a special, self-surpassing emotion—the drive and desire to overcome ignorance and attachment because of an awareness of impermanence.

The following kanshi, #33-C, one of a series of fifteen verses on Dōgen's Echizen "mountain retreat," expresses his creative ambivalence toward the tension between spiritual discipline and aesthetic feeling:

> *For so long here without worldly attachments,*
> *I have renounced literature and writing;*
> *I may be a monk in a mountain temple,*
> *Yet still moved in seeing gorgeous blossoms*
> *Scattered by the spring breeze,*
> *And hearing the warbler's lovely song—*
> *Let others judge my meager efforts.*

At the same time, it is certainly not surprising or unusual that Dōgen did experience some ambivalence concerning religion and aesthetics. An attitude of caution and misgiving about the convergence of the religious and literary traditions typified the leading Kamakura priests and writers seeking the Way. Poets whose compositions were frequently inspired by Buddhist meditation were wary of sacrificing lyrical effect for doctrinal consistency. Conversely, Buddhist monks were concerned about diminishing their spiritual purity through worldly attention to style and rhetoric. In a well-known waka by Saigyō, for example, the poet expresses ecstatic torment at being unable to avoid feeling uplifted while beholding a melancholic image of natural beauty:[30]

Kokoro naki	A heart subdued,
Mi ni mo aware wa	Yet poignant sadness
Shirarekeri	Is so deeply felt:
Shigi tatsu sawa no	A snipe flies over the marsh
Aki no yūgure.	As autumn dusk descends.

Despite the priest's better judgment, he cannot escape feeling sadness (*aware*), a response that both detracts from and enriches his spiritual state. In the following Chinese poem, Musō Soseki expresses a different sort of ambivalence. He seems to regret that his Buddhist mind is not content simply to watch the changing seasons because it insists on turning the natural setting into a metaphysical riddle or kōan:[31]

> *Autumn's colors dropping from branches in masses of falling leaves,*
> *Cold clouds bringing rain into the crannies of the mountains:*
> *Everyone was born with the same sort of eyes—*
> *Why do mine keep seeing things as Zen kōans?*

Therefore, Dōgen's struggle to reconcile religion and literature seems to be indicative of the creative tension that inspired many of the leading writers/priests of his time.

Dōgen's Convergence with Religio-Aesthetics

The convergence of Dōgen's philosophy with the religio-aesthetic tradition is based on two interrelated factors: the objective factor, or his view that ultimate reality is realized through everyday, concrete phenomena; and the subjective factor, or his emphasis on an emotional attunement to impermanence. Both Dōgen and the literati inherited the Mahayana Buddhist philosophy of nonduality, which suggests that the nothingness or emptiness of reality (Skt. *sunyata;* Chin. *wu;* Jap. *mu*) is not an abstract, idealized realm but is identical with the world of forms. The inseparability of emptiness and form is expressed in such doctrines as the Kegon "interpenetration of form and form" *(jiji muge),* the Tendai "three thousand worlds in a single instant of thought" *(ichinen sanzen)* or the "true form of all dharmas" *(shohō jissō),* Kūkai's "attaining the Buddha in this very body" *(sokushin jōbutsu),* Zen Master Ma-tsu's "this very mind itself is Buddha" *(sokushin zebutsu),* and Dōgen's own notion of impermanence-Buddha-nature: "the very impermanence of grasses and trees, thickets and forests is the Buddha-nature." From Dōgen's standpoint, each and every form, including the flowers, cuckoo, moon, and snow, neither conceals nor delimits but is in itself a manifestation of the ultimate state of reality—if and only if seen from the contemplative gaze of the casting off of body-mind. In a way that is strikingly parallel to Dōgen's approach, the poet Tamekane says of seasonal poetry, "In order to express the true nature of the natural scene, one must focus one's attention and concentrate deeply upon it.... Therefore, if you try to harmonize your feelings with the sight of cherry blossoms ... your work will become one with the very spirit of heaven and earth."[32] To write about natural phenomena, the author must cultivate a spiritual training through concentration of the mind to reach a state of genuine contemplative awareness and identification with objects that mirror his subjective realization.

Medieval Japanese literature was characterized by a sense of "depth" *(fukami)* in pursuit of art as a "way" of personal realization of the true mind *(kokoro* or *ushin)*.[33] According to literary criticism, which deals primarily with the activity of creative consciousness rather than the form and style of poems, waka composition is considered a religio-aesthetic discipline *(shugyō)*. Waka poetry, frequently derived from the Tendai Buddhist meditative practice of cessation-contemplation *(shikan)*, refines, purifies, and uplifts emotional responses to the world of form. In "Maigetsushō," for example, Fujiwara Teika asserts the priority of realizing the "original mind" *(moto no kokoro)* of serene subjectivity as the foundation or "seed" for writing waka. He interprets the words *(kotoba)* of waka poetry as the "flower" *(hana)* of art. Zeami was influenced by Dōgen's view that both actor and audience engaged in the Noh play's performance can attain subjective purity and tranquillity. According to Zeami, extending and yet reversing Teika, "the flower is the mind, the seed is the performance." That is, the realization of inner spiritual truth through aesthetic discipline (the flower) has priority over the external demonstration of art (the seed), in a way very much parallel to the training and realization of a Zen monk.

The aesthetic ideals prevalent in the medieval period of *yūgen* (profound mystery), *sabi* (loneliness or solitude), *yojō* (overtones), and *aware* (poignancy at the passing of things) do not rest on ordinary feelings or words about the seasons. Rather, they suggest a fundamental unity of humans and nature, absolute and relative, and subjectivity and objectivity. *Yūgen* generally is expressed in descriptive poetry that appears to border on realism but actually harbors a radical contemplative stance that connects the author to a formless universal truth. According to Chōmei's interpretation, *yūgen* conveys a profundity of mystery and tranquillity "only when many meanings are compressed into a single word, when the depths of feeling are exhausted yet not expressed, when an unseen world hovers in the atmosphere of the poem."[34] Shunzei compares the hovering atmosphere that is distinct from and yet accompanies words to the particular seasonal images of the "haze that trails over the cherry blossoms in spring . . . [or] the cry of the deer against the autumn moon."[35] According to Teika, the basis of composing poems that express *yūgen* must be the direct and unimpeded effusion from the true mind. Thus *yūgen* appears to be a prime example of what the preeminent Kyoto School philosopher Nishida Kitarō calls the Japanese "cultural sensitivity or lyricism" *(jōteki bunka)*, which perceives the truth of reality as "formless and voiceless" *(katachi naki, koe naki)*.[36] Formlessness and voicelessness refer to the transcendental awareness in and through yet hovering just beyond phenomena, and to the echoing, mysterious silence arising from and yet surpassing language. Because of *yūgen*'s deeply subjective basis, several modern intellectual historians have argued that the view-of-nature *(shizen-kan)* and the view-of-impermanence *(mujō-kan)* articulated in *yūgen* literature must be considered a genuine religious standpoint of self-attainment alongside Buddhism and Shinto, or in some cases as the basis of the institutional religions.

Kawabata's comments on "Original Face" highlight a convergence of the spiritual concerns and methods of Dōgen and the aims and attitudes of the religio-aesthetic tradition. In a similar vein, some critics maintain that in his poetic and prose writings, Dōgen depicts the essential meaning of viewing-impermanence and viewing-nature in terms of "existence as it is" *(arinomama)* or the "primordial and unadorned" *(rakei,* "naked" or "uncovered") level of time and nature.[37] "Original Face" can be compared with the works of *yūgen* writers who express a deeply subjective harmony with the passing of the seasons in order to penetrate to the truth of time and nature unbound by sentimentality and idle emotionalism. For example, Kenkō says, "The changing of the seasons is deeply moving in its every manifestation."[38] Dōgen's waka also recalls Chōmei's view of the seasons in *Hōjōki:* "In the spring I see waves of wisteria like purple clouds, bright in the west. In the summer I hear the cuckoo call, promising to guide me on the road of death. In the autumn the voice of the evening insect fills my ears with a sound of lamentation for this cracked husk of a world. In winter I look with deep emotion on the snow, piling up and melting away like sins and hindrances to salvation."[39] Dōgen, Kenkō, and Chōmei all see transiency in terms of the realization of the true self. While Pure Land hermit Chōmei stresses the role of sin and repentance, Zen Master Dōgen's verse raises the spiritual question of true personal identity or the ultimate nature of the self, evoking Hui-neng's query "What is the look on your face before your were born?" On the one hand, "Original Face" is a simple description of four cyclically recurring natural forms, each frequently celebrated in Japanese literature. Yet the poem is in accord with the aim of *yūgen* in conveying a profound subjectivity through descriptive symbolism. The spontaneous linking of images suggests the truth of the impermanence of nature, at once undermining the stability and heightening the ephemeral beauty of any particular seasonal manifestation. This symbolizes the enlightenment realization discussed in the *Shōbōgenzō* "Genjōkōan" (Spontaneous realization of the kōan) saying "To study the self is to forget the self and realize the truth through all phenomena."

The relation between the personal and universal aspects of Dōgen's view is also expressed in the first poem in his waka collection, #1-J, which is perhaps his most moving poem on several levels. This verse, like #2-J, concerns Dōgen's final journey to Kyoto, after ten years in Echizen, to seek medical treatment for the ailments that would cause his death shortly after his arrival at the capital. These two poems, along with a Chinese death verse, provide an insight into Dōgen's feelings near the end of his life. They represent a rare type of expression in his writings, which makes the poetry collection as a whole especially valuable. The diction and syntax of the verse #1-J play off the traditional poetic theme of travel and the imagery of evanescence to convey Dōgen's dual sense of exhilaration and anxiety, and expectation and frailty during the trip:

Kusa no ha ni	*Like a blade of grass,*
Kadodeseru mi no	*My frail body*
Kinobe yama	*Treading the path to Kyoto,*
Kumo ni oka aru	*Seeming to wander*
Kokochi koso sure.	*Amid the cloudy mist on*
	Kinobe Pass.

Kusa no ha (a blade of grass) is a multidimensional image. First, it connotes travel *(tabi)*, a theme used generally in Court poetry to suggest someone's feeling of either dismay or relief in leaving Kyoto, but here it ironically expresses uneasiness about an imminent return. On a symbolic level, the image indicates the fragility and vulnerability that pervades yet undercuts the existence of each and every being. It also recalls several passages in the *Shōbōgenzō* in which Dōgen equates "the radiance of a hundred blades of grass" with the true nature of reality, or maintains that "a single blade of grass and a single tree are both the body-mind of all Buddhas."[40] *Kusa no ha* therefore expresses a convergence of departure and return, feeling and detachment, and particularity and frailty with the universal nonsubstantiality of phenomena.

Another important image in the poem involves the word *oka*, which literally means "hill" and makes an association with Kinobe *yama* (*yama* or "mountain" here actually means "Pass" in "Kinobe Pass," a steep precipice Dōgen had to cross midway between Eiheiji and Kyoto). The syllable *ka* (questioning) also conveys Dōgen's deep uncertainty about, yet his feeling of, a fleeting moment of liberation from his current medical condition, as his spirit seems to float and feels lost in the clouds. He at once transcends his physical problems and realizes he can never be free from the travails of impermanence. The alliteration of *k*s at the beginning of each line adds a solemn or reverent undertone, while the word *kokochi* (a synonym for *kokoro,* heart/mind) softens the sentiment or transmutes it into an expression of subjective realization. The mind appears to be released, although the "body" *(mi)* is bound by suffering. One critic, Ōba Nanboku, who wrote the main modern commentary on the waka collection, further suggests that the image of clouds recalls the Zen doctrine of training for enlightenment as "floating like the clouds, flowing like the water" *(unsui).*[41] Thus the poem represents a transformation of a personal sentiment and an aesthetic perception into a holistic experience of liberation.

The Role of Emotions in Aesthetic Awareness

There are numerous poems in Dōgen's collections of verse that express the belief that an aesthetic attunement to the forms of nature is compatible with or even essential for religious truth. Waka #8-J, composed in the first autumn of Dōgen's stay in Echizen, is notable not so much as elegant poetry (the imagery seems derivative) but as a direct statement of Dōgen's view of the spiritual importance of emotion and intuition:

Nagazuki no	Crimson leaves
Momiji no ue ni	Whitened by the season's first snow—
Yuki furinu	Is there anyone
Minhito tareka	Who would not be moved
Uta o yomazaran.	To celebrate this in song?

Here the striking beauty of contrasting and interspersed hues highlighting the transition of seasons inspires a moment of poetic rapture. The waka reveals a convergence of individual sentiment with the arising of a universal aesthetic perception, and it recalls the opening lines of Ki no Tsurayuki's famous preface to the *Kokinshū*, which remains the essential statement of Japanese literary criticism:[42]

> The poetry of Japan takes hold in the heart of humans and springs forth in the innumerable petals of words. Because of humans' intense involvement in the world, it is poetry that expresses the inner feeling of his heart upon viewing the sights of the world and hearing its sounds. To hear a nightingale singing amidst the blossoms or a frog croaking in the water—is there anyone alive who would not be moved to celebrate this in song?

Dōgen seems to concur with Tsurayuki that an undeniable impulse toward poetic creativity makes itself felt in one's consciousness, like a natural force that inevitably flourishes in response to the seasons and elements. A prime example of Dōgen's poetic use of language in his prose writings to express aesthetic emotion occurs in the opening paragraph of "Genjōkōan," which appears as the introductory fascicle in most editions. In the first several sentences Dōgen repeats the Mahayana theme of the non-differentiability of apparent opposites such as delusion and enlightenment, life and death, and Buddhas and sentient beings. In the final sentence he writes, "And yet, even though this has been said, blossoms scatter in sadness and weeds spring up in dismay."[43] This sentence is echoed in kanshi verse #5-C:

> *Flowers falling even as we turn our admiring gaze,*
> *While weeds keep springing up despite our chagrin.*

The "Genjōkōan" sentence, like the kanshi verse, is so rich in its brevity and ambiguous in its lyrical imagery of seasonal change that it can be seen as representing a variety of perspectives. These primarily include either an implicit critique of emotional attachment to forms or the evocation of a religio-aesthetic awareness of the interrelatedness of human feeling and natural surroundings. One interpretation suggests that the sentence advocates the need for humans to thoroughly negate their emotions, which egoistically and self-defeatingly produce the contingent flux of existence by perpetuating volitional bondage to transient entities. The limitation in this reading of the passage, however, is that the emotional response to transiency is seen as the actual cause of impermanence. Emotions do not create the pervasive and perpetual process of change, although it is true that when a person does not comprehend the nonsubstantive ground of transiency, emotions may aggravate suffering. Yet the distinction between cause and response, or evanescence and self-imposed bondage, must be highlighted.

A religio-aesthetic interpretation argues that the "Genjōkōan" sentence demonstrates a transcendental view at once encompassing and sublating the human emotions of sorrow and grief over the transiency of nature. Genuine spiritual realization must be found by embracing—rather than by eliminating—one's emotional response to variability and inevitable loss. The poignantly moved heart *(kokoro)*, which feels "sadness" *(aijaku)* and "dismay" *(kiken)*, undergoes a feeling of turmoil and anguish in the face of change. This level of awareness is crucial for stirring the mind to pursue enlightenment because it discloses an overriding moral impulse to terminate the suffering of self and others based on an underlying identification with the ephemeral fate of all natural phenomena. Such an interpretation appears more comprehensive than the previous one, for it suggests the intimate connection between form and subjectivity, lyricism, and true realization. Thus the "Genjōkōan" sentence expresses a double-edged sense of dejection and despair or of longing and aspiration in pursuit of liberation—attitudes that must be either uprooted or cultivated even while it must be acknowledged that they cannot alter the fundamental course of events or resist the incessancy of change. "Genjōkōan" thereby provides a lyrical evocation of the subtly contrasting shades and textures of the emotional struggle to realize and overcome sorrow. It does not state a truth that is reducible to formula but aesthetically conveys the disturbing and inspiring encounters at the basis of the quest for truth.

Waka #51-J similarly stresses that grief has a role to play in the acceptance of natural change and that grief can be a source of religious aspiration:

> *Kokoro naki*   *Even plants and trees,*
> *Kusaki mo kyō wa*   *Which have no heart,*
> *Shibomu nari*   *Wither with the passing days;*
> *Me ni mitaru hito*   *Beholding this,*
> *Ure-e zarameya.*   *Can anyone help but feel chagrin?*

As all beings are interrelated by virtue of the transiency that invariably undercuts their apparent stability, humans necessarily respond to the demise of plants and trees "which have no heart" *(kokoro naki)*. The latter phrase is used in Court poetry, as in the Saigyō verse cited above, to denote a priest with a subdued heart, or one who has conquered any attachment to feelings through meditation. In Dōgen's verse, the phrase carries at least a double message. The plants can be considered to lack an awareness of their plight due to either a subhuman absence of consciousness or a symbolic suprahuman transcendence of sorrowful emotions based on an innate acceptance of the natural situation. At the same time, the priest implicitly referred to by the phrase cannot avoid feeling chagrin *(ure-e)* despite his apparent state of liberation. Or, rather, the aesthetic perception—or the awakening of an aesthetically attuned heart—dislodges even a priest's clinging to the view that perishability is something objective and apart from one's own existence by highlighting the way it pervades subjectivity. Therefore, the refined emotion of sorrow is more conducive than strict detachment to exploring the existential depths of enlightenment. Dōgen's approach to evoking the ephemeral quality of humans and nature symbolically has been compared with the following poem by Fujiwara Teika, an allusive variation of an earlier waka by Tomonori:[44]

Ika ni shite	What reason is there
Shizugokoro naku	That these cherry petals fluttering
Chiru hana no	With such unsettled heart
Nodokeki haru no	Should symbolize the essential color
Iro to miyu ran.	Of the soft tranquillity of spring?

There are differences between Teika, the Court poet, and Dōgen, the seeker of the Way. But Teika's commitment to composing waka based on a contemplative realization infused "with-mind" resembles Dōgen's approach in that both authors penetrate to the most fundamental or primordial level of nature. On the one hand, the two waka are nearly opposite in that Dōgen sees plants as devoid of feeling while Teika projects onto the cherry blossoms the all-too-human sense of a restless heart. Yet each poem points to the intimate connection and empathetic sensitivity of humans in communion with the phenomena of nature, as well as the interrelated feelings of instability or grief and tranquillity or transcendence. An aesthetic response to forms is essential to the attainment of an authentic subjectivity and a creative, self-illuminating awareness that is immersed in nature and that goes beyond the vacillations of personal emotions.

A key aspect of aesthetic attunement is selecting language that is appropriate for expressing emotions. Waka #26-J, one of several poems in Dōgen's collection that deal explicitly with the issue of language and symbol in communicating the Buddhist Dharma, discloses the fundamental link between speech and impermanence in Dōgen's approach to Zen. The poem revolves around the pivot-word *koto no ha* (petals of words), which includes the preposition *no* (of) in the term *kotoba* (language). This wordplay, also used in Tsurayuki's *Kokinshū* preface cited previously, offers an alternative pronunciation and meaning of the ordinary word, thus indicating a deeper level of significance: the countless manifestations, rising and falling, of human discourse. *Koto no ha* here makes an association with *hana no uta* (flower's song):

> Haru kaze ni
> Waga koto no ha no
> Chirinuru o
>
> Hana no uta to ya
> Hito no nagamen.

> Will their gaze fall upon
> The petals of words I utter,
> Shaken loose and blown free by the
>   spring breeze,
> As if only the notes
> Of a flower's song?

The poem can be understood on two levels. First, Dōgen implicitly criticizes the average perspective, which sees language as a mere ornament or artifice fluttering about like shimmery spring blossoms. At the same time he suggests that this limited awareness fails to realize the more primary association between words and flowers. That is, the transiency of discourse, symbolized by the outpouring of expression, is identical to the scattering of blossoms; it is enhanced and opposed, inspired and restrained, by the vicissitudes of the spring breeze. Discourse is itself a full and concrete manifestation of the reality of impermanence and the unity of humans and nature. Words attain their meaning in the same way flowers realize their beauty—because of their frailty and evanescence. The use of personification in the image of the "flower's song" indicates that the ephemeral beauty of the blossom is reciting a tale of sadness and regret, which is the fundamental message of the sutras and sayings in articulating the Dharma.

Re-rendering "Original Face"

Following from these points, it is possible to rethink Seidensticker's translation of "Original Face." The aesthetic configuration of the waka, which complements its religious aspect, is primarily based on the multiple nuances of the adjective *suzushi* appearing in the final line. *Suzushi* can be taken to mean, as Seidensticker's version indicates, the physical characteristic or bodily sensation of the brightness and coldness of the snow. Yet that rendering, which suggests that *suzushi* merely amplifies *kiede* (frozen) in modifying *snow*, represents but one level of meaning. In Court poetry *suzushi* often implies the serene and cool outlook—encompassing both objective appearance and subjective response—generated by phenomena that are not literally cold. The term is used by Tamekane, for instance, to describe the purity and coolness of the voice of the cuckoo *(hototogisu)*, a synesthesia that illustrates the underlying and complex interrelatedness of personal reaction and external stimulus, body and mind, and sensation and awareness.[45] *Suzushi* refers to neither just the snow nor the observer, to neither the physical nor the mental. Rather, it suggests a lyricism that is rooted and yet unlimited by the forms previously portrayed in the poem.

In this context, Ōba's interpretation argues that Dōgen uses the word *suzushi* in a religio-aesthetic way to comment on human involvement in seasonal interpenetration, or the immediate and renewable response to the perpetual rotation of four distinct yet overlapping phenomena.[46] Thus *suzushi* reflects the lyricism of the entire poem, expressing the primordial unity encompassing infinite diversity and the possibility for momentary change by modifying each of the seasonal images: the vivid colors and graceful scattering of spring flowers, the sharp cry of the cuckoo at dawn or dusk, the clarity and tranquillity of autumn moonlight, and the purity of freshly fallen snow. *Suzushi* is not just another modifier in a descriptive poem otherwise noted for being nearly devoid of adjectives. On the other hand, it does not imply a conventional feeling by a subject that reacts to an objectified stimulus, though this level of meaning should not be excluded from the interpretation. Rather *suzushi* refers to nature in and of itself—or nature "as it is"—in such a way that subjectivity neither interferes with nor is severed from the holistic and impersonal manifestation of each and every phenomenon. That is, the subject is symbolically removed from the setting as an independent entity to return to or participate in the cyclical unity. Thus *suzushi* expresses the poem's central, consistent transcendental attitude toward the entire array of images, in which a peak aspect of nature is perfectly reflected by one who experiences reality as it is.

An alternative translation, also supported by the ending word *keri,* which represents an affirmation of the beauty of the season, reads:

Honrai no memmoku	*Original Face*
Haru wa hana	*In spring, the cherry blossoms,*
Natsu hototogisu	*In summer, the cuckoo's song,*
Aki wa tsuki	*In autumn, the moon, shining,*
Fuyu yuki kiede	*In winter, the frozen snow:*
Suzushi kari keri.	*How pure and clear are the seasons!*

CHAPTER TWO

Dewdrops on a Blade of Grass: Poetic Themes

THE STRUCTURE of Dōgen's poetry collections can be analyzed in two ways. One way, which will be discussed in the following two chapters as a means of introducing the translations, is to group together the poems in the Japanese and the Chinese collections by common styles or dates of composition. The other mode of analysis, explained in this chapter, is to examine poetic themes that are prevalent in a number of waka and kanshi verses. Dōgen's poems reflect a variety of thematic elements. While his primary aim in writing verse was almost certainly didactic or instructional, some of the more creative verses may be appreciated for their subtle and refined lyrical imagery and aesthetic themes. Several effectively use intricate waka conceits, though a number of others are quite direct in their diction. Yet the verses that seem less inspired from a strictly literary standpoint often exhibit other levels of significance in terms of what they reveal about Dōgen's life or the beliefs and practices he exhibited in his approach to Zen. Furthermore, a number of poems can be interpreted on more than one level because Dōgen uses imagery usually associated with poetic feelings of longing or loneliness to express his religious views or personal experiences. The categories developed here, which are by no means hard-and-fast, mutually exclusive distinctions, point out three main themes: 1.) lyrical poetry, which uses natural imagery to convey an aesthetic emotional quality that is related to a sensitivity to transiency; 2.) didactic poetry, which is primarily instructive in key aspects of Buddhist philosophy also explored in the *Shōbōgenzō,* such as overcoming illusion by realizing authentic subjectivity through attaining an awareness of the impermanence of nature, and practicing meditation and devotionalism; and 3.) personal poetry, which focuses on Dōgen's reactions to events or his attitudes about experiences, especially regarding the relation between monasticism and society. The central, underlying thread in all three categories is Dōgen's concern with the meaning of the contemplative life and its expression through daily activities, including literary composition.

Lyrical Poems

Perhaps the finest poems in Dōgen's collections are those that demonstrate multiple levels of significance, especially when the lyrical meaning enhances personal or didactic elements, which in turn do not impede but refine the literary quality. In waka #19-J, one of a series of verses composed for delivery to the shogun in Kamakura in 1247, the image of a small boat drifting in the light of the midnight moon at once suggests an aesthetic state of solitude, the doctrine of casting off body-mind, and Dōgen's personal sense of aloofness during a journey to the Five Mountains Rinzai center:

Shōbōgenzō	*Treasury of the true Dharma-eye*
Nami mo hiki	*In the heart of the night,*
Kaze mo tsunaganu	*The moonlight framing*

Sute obune	A *small boat drifting,*
Tsuki koso yawa no	*Tossed not by the waves*
Sakai nari keri.	*Nor swayed by the breeze.*

The phrase *sute obune* (lit. "boat that has been cast out") conventionally signifies loneliness or alienation in an impersonal world, but it is transformed here into a symbol of the strength, detachment, and dedication required in the search for enlightenment. The "drifting boat" is not at the mercy of the elements but appears to be thoroughly undisturbed by the "waves" (symbolizing objects of attachment) and the "breeze" (ignorance and desire). Because the verb *suteru* (to be cast out or to renounce) is frequently used by Dōgen interchangeably with *datsuraku* (lit. "letting go of"), the expression *sute obune* seems to represent the casting off of bodymind *(shinjin datsuraku).*

The image of illumination by the moon has connotations from the poetic tradition, in which it represents an object of longing and the source of comfort in times of turmoil and grief, as well as Buddhist implications as the symbol of the universal manifestations of the compassion and wisdom of Buddha-nature. The moon deepens the meaning of the resolute detachment of the casting off of the boat. The boat is cut off from the harbor, as perhaps Dōgen felt isolated during his trip to the Five Mountains Rinzai center. But because the boat falls within the encompassment of the moon's glow, it is not lost but protected by the compassionate Buddha-nature. Yet in contrast to the moon, the boat is not totally aloof from the world of variability; it remains involved, at once aimless in its solitude and purposeful in its disciplined response to change. The single phenomenon of the drifting boat shares the detached perspective and illuminative remoteness of the moonlight, and partakes of the world into which it has been cast out, yet has learned to cast off perpetually.

Another example of highly suggestive, evocative lyricism in support of a religious message is waka #28-J, which relies on conceits of the poetic tradition to heighten the impact of its devotional theme. This poem about Buddhist worship weaves together a relational word and the imagery of an intimate love affair with the themes of travel and homage paying to create a syntactical effect that is beyond its component parts and a message only hinted at by the literal sense of the words:

Tanomi koshi	A *traveler in Echizen,*
Mukashi no shū ya	*Wrapping my sorrow with a linen sleeve:*
Yūdasuki	*My plea that I be veiled*
Aware o kakeyo	*By the compassion*
Asa no sode ni mo.	*Of the original Lord.*

The poem is centered on the double meaning of *aware* as "sorrow" and "compassion," and its relation to the association between *asa no sode* (linen sleeve) and the phrase *yūdasuki . . . o kakeyo* (lit. "tucking up [one's sleeve] with a sash"). On one level, the last three lines in the original suggest a sense of grief or bereavement owing to the loss of a loved one by either circumstance or perhaps death. The term *linen sleeve* adds a touch of refinement and elegance to the image of someone unfolding his sorrow as if it were an exquisite garment, at once concealing and displaying the sentiment.

The feeling of loss is deepened and somewhat altered by the image in the opening lines of a wearying journey undertaken in order to beseech or offer a plea *(tanomi),* perhaps for forgiveness or relief from suffering. *Koshi* is a pivot-word that means both "crossing" and the "thick" or "dark" entanglements of an obstructed roadway; it is also the first character of the name "Echizen," suggesting travel to the remote mountain province of Dōgen's temple, the trip being frequently celebrated in Court poetry as a way of escaping the capital. The travel image plays off the second meaning of *aware,* evoking a solemn atmosphere, indicating that the bereaved not only wraps up his sorrow but has journeyed to request that he be enveloped in or veiled by the compassion of a forgiving power, *mukashi no shū* (lit. "lord of old"). The term for the object of the plea conjures up a feudal lord or, more likely, a Shinto deity, accentuated by the allusion to the ritualistic draping of a priest's shoulder scarf *(yūdasuki)*. The combined effect is to convey a twofold image of one who, in offering respect and sorrow in beseeching the lord, receives the grace of compassion, just as the feudal lord accepts the plea and bestows his favor. Although the poem does not mention the Buddha and, in fact, depends upon non-Buddhist lyrical and religious imagery, it clearly evokes the interaction between Buddha and disciple—an aesthetic relation of intimate embracing in which both parties simultaneously bestow and receive the other's blessing. Dōgen thus uses waka conventions to disclose the fundamental act of Buddhist practice, bypassing the traditional dichotomy between self-power *(jiriki),* associated with Zen meditation, and other-power *(tariki)* of Pure Land worship. The poem suggests the doctrine of "reciprocal spiritual communion between master and disciple" *(kannō-dōkō)* referred to in the *Shōbōgenzō,* so that each party enlightens the other without there being a hierarchical distinction between the two.

Other waka in which lyricism seems to outweigh and yet sustains the doctrinal or personal meaning of the poem include #1-J and 2-J on Dōgen's sense of frailty and longing during his final journey to Kyoto; #6-J, which anthropomorphically identifies Sakyamuni with the mountains and valleys; #9-J and 26-J, which use intricate wordplay to divulge the full potentiality of language in relation to the Dharma; #13-J and the sequence 37-J–40-J on the mysterious depths of mountain travel and solitude; #25-J, 40-J, 50-J, and 60-J, which, respectively, use the seasonal imagery of a cicada announcing the approach of autumn twilight, the fading sunlight of early spring, and the evaporating dew and firefly's light of late summer to reveal poignantly the pervasiveness of impermanence and nonsubstantiality; #34-J on an ambivalent attraction to natural forms; and #61-J on the interplay of universality and particularity symbolized by moonlight reflected in dewdrops.

Many of the Chinese kanshi are also primarily lyrical, including #10-C, which alludes to a traditional Buddhist parable that is especially popular in Japan, suggesting that at the time of Buddha's death and attainment of parinirvana a bright forest lost its color as all living creatures grieved the loss, while a crane, symbolizing immortality, continued its heavenly flight, unperturbed:

> *In the dead of the night,*
> *The moon low in the sky,*
> *As Sakyamuni enters parinirvana,*
> *The jade forest, turning white,*
> *Cannot play host to*
> *A thousand-year-old crane,*
> *Whose glistening feathers*
> *Fly right by the empty nest.*

There is an interesting contrast in that the Chinese poem emphasizes timelessness conquering death, or at least suggests a realm beyond mortality, also symbolized by the pines and bamboo that endure a harsh climate with a sense of nobility as in kanshi #11-C, 23-C, and 27-C, whereas Japanese verses invariably evoke the inalterability of transiency.

In waka #50-J, the image of the dew (*tsuyu*; lit. "dewdrops," also suggesting "tears"), like the moon in #19-J, suggests the flux of time, an idea that resonates in both the Buddhist and the poetic traditions:

Asahi matsu	Dewdrops on a blade of grass,
Kusaba no tsuyu no	Having so little time
Hodonaki ni	Before the sun rises;
Isogina tachi so	Let not the autumn wind
Nobe no akikaze.	Blow so quickly on the field.

Here the dew epitomizes the fleeting quality of all things, showing that all things are manifestations of the universal structure of life-death and arising-desistance. In waka #47-J, Dōgen uses the image of "dew-frost" (*tsuyu-jimo*) to indicate that the nonsubstantiality of body and mind is identical to the transiency of natural elements. The aim in expressing a metaphysical understanding of impermanence in #50-J is to send an implicit moral message. Dōgen chides the wind for causing the evaporation of the dew, in order to counsel disciples to neither resist nor waste time, which flows at an ever quickening pace. People, who are subject to the same laws that govern the dew, must seize the opportunity to take advantage of the fleeting but complete here-and-now moments that recur in the inevitable movement from life to death. Moral practice and metaphysical insight are based on an aesthetic sensitivity to and sympathy with the precariousness and vulnerability of natural phenomena. Dōgen's poem recalls Chōmei's introduction to the *Hōjōki:* "Which will be the first to go, the master or his dwelling? One might just as well ask this of the dew on the morning glory. The dew may fall and the flower remain—remain, only to be withered by the morning sun. The flower may fade before the dew evaporates, but though it does not evaporate, it waits not the evening."[1] It is the emotional identification with the plight of evanescent things, and the consequent anguish and outrage, that awakens the need for release from suffering. Enlightenment is attained as empathetic grief is transformed into a realization of the nonsubstantive basis of existence.

    Dōgen's elegant lyrical verse indicates that his religious vision incorporates a constellation of at least six interrelated factors that are symbolized by the "dew," which will be examined in the following section. Dewdrops, a conventional epithet for autumn, represent the transient, *impermanent* foundations of *nature* reflected in the changing of the seasons. As Kenkō writes, "If man were never to fade away like the dews of Adashino, never to vanish like the smoke over Toribeyama, but lingered on forever in the world, how things would lose their power to move us! The most precious thing in life is its uncertainty."[2] In evoking "tears," *tsuyu* suggests the inseparability of *emotions* and insight, or the essential connection between sadness and awakening, as eloquently described in #23-C. Dew also represents the *illusory* status of the "floating world." Like dreams, mirages, bubbles, and so forth, dew is a symbol of the relativity of illusion and truth based on the nonsubstantive or radically impermanent ground of existence. The multiple implications of *tsuyu* also highlight the important role poetic *symbolism* plays here in portraying transcendent levels of awareness, including *devotionalism* bypassing the self-power/other-power distinction.

Doctrinal Poems

The poems in the doctrinal category often make an interesting use of poetic imagery and stylistic conventions but are noteworthy mainly for their didacticism. For example, waka #30-J seems to be an allusive variation on a famous love poem attributed to Hitomaro and included in several noted anthologies such as Teika's *Hyakunin isshu* and *Kindai shūka*. The original verse conveys the nightlong torment of unrequited love that leaves one unable to sleep. It uses the pillow-word *ashihiki* to modify *mountain*, in that "pheasant" is literally a "mountain bird" *(yamadori)* in the first three lines, which provide the setting for the evocation of loneliness and despair in the last two lines:

Ashihiki no	Long night,
Yamadori no o no	Long as the
Shidario no	Long tail of the pheasant:
Naganagashi yo o	I find myself here
Hitori ka mo nen.	Resting alone.

Borrowing the opening lines of this poem so that some of the implications of the original are suggested, Dōgen turns the verse into an expression of the doctrine of the identity of "original enlightenment and marvelous sustained practice" *(honshō myōshū)*:

Ashihiki no	Long night,
Yamadori no o no	Long as the
Shidario no	Long tail of the pheasant:

> *Naganagashi yo mo* The light of dawn
> *Akete keri kana.* Breaking through.

The image of imminent daybreak is implied in the source poem in the traditional sense of suggesting the sad parting of lovers, or more poignantly here, in a heightened awareness of the partner's absence. In Dōgen's version, however, the dawn explicitly and positively connotes the sudden appearance of self-illumination, an effective metaphor for Zen awakening, evoking the event of Sakyamuni's enlightenment after his nightly vigils. The new poem conveys the interplay of delusion (night) and realization (dawn), and meditation (the "long" night of practice) and awakening (the disclosure of light), to show the unity underlying the different phases and the gradual unfolding of the enlightenment experience. Yet this waka can be criticized for using too much of the original verse; the device of variation tends to be more effective if the echoing is somewhat more concealed by the syntax.

Some other examples in which conventional wordplay and imagery are used for didactic reasons include the relational word *shiranami* in #17-J, creating an association between "white waves" and "seagull," in contrast to the spotted duck, to illustrate the nondistinction of appearance and reality; the image of spring blossoms in #11-J, 20-J, and 27-J, which deal with the relation between impermanence and eternity; the alliteration of *k*'s in #3-J to indicate that "this *{Lotus} Sutra*" *(kono kyō)* and the "voice and heart" *(koe to kokoro)* are neither separable entities nor collapsed into a monolithic uniformity but exist in an intimate and dynamic rapport that reverberates throughout the manifestations of impermanence; and the natural imagery of #15-J and 18-J, used to convey the spontaneous or effortless exertion of continuous enlightenment.

A kanshi verse, #16-C, which accompanies one of two famous portraits of Dōgen, uses an intricate wordplay involving the word *real* to make a statement about the inseparability of truth and illusion:

> *If you take this portrait of me to be real,*
> *Then what am I, really?*
> *But why hang it there,*
> *If not to anticipate people getting to know me?*
> *Looking at this portrait,*
> *Can you say that what is hanging there*
> *Is really me?*
> *In that case your mind will never be*
> *Fully united with the wall {as in Bodhidharma's wall-gazing*
> *meditation cave}.*

The last line alludes to the first patriarch's practice of zazen while gazing at the wall of a cave for nine years. There is a delightful, self-deprecatory irony in this verse, given the important ritual role portraits play in Zen monastic life as objects of veneration, substituting for a deceased master on ceremonial occasions, a convention Dōgen obviously questions but does not necessarily reject.

As suggested above, the doctrinal poems can be analyzed in terms of the way in which they suggest key aspects of Dōgen's overall philosophy of religion as expressed in the *Shōbōgenzō*, as well as show affinities with the religio-aesthetic tradition.

Impermanence

The background theme for the majority of doctrinal poems is the meaning of impermanence, the fundamental concern in Dōgen's life and thought. This issue, central to all forms of Buddhist philosophy, also marks the basic point of convergence between Dōgen and the literary tradition. According to biographical sources, Dōgen's understanding of impermanence was based on a childhood feeling of anguish and abandonment because of the death of his parents, symbolized by the smoke drifting from the incense at his mother's funeral. Although the traditional account may be exaggerated, it is clear that the deep sense of sorrow Dōgen experienced

figure 4. *Dōgen's Portrait*

This portrait of Dōgen, on which is inscribed Chinese poem #16-C, was done at Kōshōji Temple for ceremonial purposes, which Dōgen's verse calls into question.

lies at the root of his philosophy of the unity of practice and realization. Inspired by his grief, Dōgen stresses the need for continuous meditation renewed each and every moment right here and now.

In *Shōbōgenzō zuimonki,* Dōgen argues repeatedly that "the first and foremost thing to be concerned with is detachment from the ego through the contemplation of impermanence." The notion that coming to terms with impermanence is crucial to the abandonment of egocentrism is also stressed in the following passage in *Gakudōyōjinshū,* which Kyoto School intellectual historian Karaki Junzō cites as exemplifying Japanese lyrical eloquence about transiency. Here Dōgen emphasizes that the aspiration to attain enlightenment and the transformation of the self occur only when impermanence is authentically understood:[3]

> When you contemplate impermanence genuinely, the ordinary selfish mind does not arise, and you do not seek fame or fortune because you realize that nothing prevents the swift flow of time. You must practice the Way as though you were trying to keep your head from being consumed by fire. . . . If you hear the flattering call of the god Kimnara or the kalavinka bird, regard them as merely the breeze blowing in your ears. Even though you see the beautiful face of Mao-ch'ing or Hsi-shih, consider that they are the morning dew obstructing your vision.

Dōgen distinguishes between two perspectives: the inauthentic or selfish view, which negates or overlooks impermanence and presumes the stability of worldly concerns; and the enlightened standpoint of non-ego, in which a person's awareness of the fleeting quality of time transmutes into a resolve for perpetual training. An authentic view of impermanence, according to Dōgen, leads one to identify practice and realization with the holistic moment that encompasses self and other, as well as the three tenses of time. Transiency is seen not as a barrier or obstacle to attainment but as the vehicle by which enlightenment is realized and renewed. In *Shōbōgenzō* "Bendōwa" (Discussing the practice of the Way) he maintains, "Even if practiced by only a single person at one time, zazen imperceptibly reverberates throughout every dharma at all times. Therefore, it ceaselessly transmits the Buddha's teaching in the past, present and future of the entire unlimited universe."[4] Impermanence as the very structure of reality must not be resisted but embraced through a sustained awareness of the formlessness of all forms.

The theme of time and impermanence has long been dominant in Japanese literature. Poems from the era of the *Manyōshū* collection in the Nara period, including Hitomaro's long verse *(chōka)* on the discovery of a body washed up on shore and Okura's *chōka* "On the Instability of Human Life" explore the issues of grief and sadness about the transiency of life and the inevitability of death in a way that probably already reflects a Buddhist sensitivity. Okura's poem concludes by contrasting the apparent stability of nature (which is "immovable as a rock") with the unstoppability of the passing of time in the world of human concerns. The poets in the Heian era contributing to the *Kokinshū* explore the meaning of time on a whole new level by describing the fading blossoms and evaporating dew as symbolic of the metaphysical reality of impermanence encompassing humans and nature. The poets Komachi, Tsurayuki, Tomonori, and Narihara no longer presuppose that there is a distinction between the human and natural worlds. Since both realms are governed by an inalterable flux, nature's evanescence perfectly mirrors the emotional responses of affirmation and acceptance, remorse and regret, generated in the self over time. In this period of poetry, time, according to Brower and Miner, is the fundamental theme "since it is the ground and being of almost all the literature of the age. The poets often wrote of time, but it is less a subject than a condition of reality that involves poet and subject matter, poet and other men, theme, and attitude."[5]

The *monogatari* literature of the Heian period also features time as the substance and framework for creating thematic unity.

Genji monogatari, for example, uses poignant images associated with the changing of the seasons to convey the ideal of *mono no aware,* which is the feeling of longing and sorrow based on the recognition that all beautiful things and emotions, especially love, must soon pass away. Throughout the tale there runs "a preoccupation with evanescence and death. . . . One after another, the characters sicken and die, leaving the survivors with an ever deeper sense of the transience of worldly things."[6] In the Kamakura period, the opening lines of *Heike monogatari* evoke the impermanence underlying human struggles and passions through the imagery of the dying of flowers that once flourished, the brevity of springtime dreams, and the dust that is cast about by the winds of destiny.

Medieval Japanese literature goes beyond mere sentimentality in capturing the more subtle and refined emotions at the ground of the experience of impermanence. But it is the *yūgen* literature of the poets and critics who contributed to the *Shinkokinshū* in the Kamakura period that reaches a new level, particularly with some of Dōgen's contemporaries, including Shunzei, Teika, Saigyō, and Chōmei. Largely based on the meditative practice of cessation-contemplation *(shikan),* impermanence is experienced by *yūgen* writers in terms of the attainment of the true mind *(ushin)* unbound by artifice and distraction. Teika recommends that waka should be composed only when "one is fully immersed in the unique realm of the serene composure and concentration of the mind."[7] The serenity of the *yūgen* ideal does not bemoan or resist time. Time is the key not to the problems but to the resolution of existence. *Yūgen* poetry views nature as redemptive because the state of solitude or desolation in the midst of natural surroundings purifies and liberates ordinary feelings about change. The supreme value of loneliness is expressed in Jakuren's waka:[8]

> *Loneliness—*
> *The essential color of a beauty*
> *Not to be defined:*
> *Over the dark evergreens, the dusk*

That gathers on far autumn hills.

Here, solitude *(sabi)* becomes a healing experience that embraces impermanence in its most fundamental and unadorned meaning without emotional vacillation.

Impermanence for both Dōgen, as reflected in the majority of his verses on the transition of the seasons, and the literary tradition is intimately related to the emotions and the issue of illusion. Impermanence necessarily elicits a personal response, because change and variability affect self-identity. The attitude that is generated in the person or subject concerning the evanescence of the natural or objective world may be based either on sensing transiency because of experiences of sadness and loss, or introspectively reflecting on its significance through contemplation. As the contemplative stance develops, ordinary emotions are surpassed by means of an impersonal and holistic insight into the nonsubstantive structure of reality. Yet contemplation does not negate the emotions altogether, and the relation between the contemplative and emotional perspectives is variable and complex. Understanding the instability that coexists with impermanence also leads to a concern with illusion since the status of self and things is fundamentally challenged. In this world of floating dreams and evaporating dew, the question becomes, Is there anything enduring and "really real"? Kenkō writes, "The world is a place of such uncertainty and change that what we imagine we see before our eyes really does not exist. . . . External things are all illusions. Does anything remain unaltered even for the shortest time?"[9] The degree to which the question of illusion is resolved depends on the level of subjectivity attained in reflecting on the meaning of impermanence.

Emotions

Thus emotions, or subjectivity, is a key to interpreting the main similarities and differences between Dōgen the religious seeker and medieval literature based on *yūgen*. According to Karaki's analysis, the high point in the development of the view of impermanence in Japanese intellectual history is the overcoming of any trace of emotionalism in Dōgen's religious thought. Dōgen casts off inauthentic deceptions and fixations through a complete acceptance of impermanence in its fundamental state. He asserts, for example, that the identity of "birth-death, and arising-desistance, is itself [nothing other than] *nirvana*." In contrast, Japanese poetry, as Robert Brower and Earl Miner suggest, considers that "the great enemy of nature and human affairs is time . . . [for time] is a force over which man has no control at all."[10] Yet to dispute Karaki's conclusion, at least in part, Dōgen's poetry does resemble literary expressions in that it shows a remarkable range of emotions, from the celebration of moments of ephemeral beauty to the expression of loneliness, longing, and regret. At the same time, *yūgen* poetry expressing *sabi* completes the emotional cycle in emphasizing melancholic resignation or desolation.

Transiency for Dōgen and the religio-aesthetic tradition can be interpreted either "negatively" as a source of suffering, grief, despair, and desolation, or "positively," as a source of celebration of the promise of renewal and as a symbol of awakening. Although transiency ultimately discloses nonsubstantiality, the subjective attitudes it evokes serve as a kind of necessary illusion or an illusion surpassing illusion in the quest for a transcendental standpoint. The "negative" view of impermanence includes Dōgen's personal lament for the loss of his parents in waka #31-J, and the poignant sorrow at the passing of things represented by the fading spring light in #40-J and the cicada's melancholy call in #25-J. The latter poem recalls the Kokinshū era with its use of the pivot-word *higurashi,* meaning "cicada," but also suggesting the setting sun *(higure),* the message the insect's sound conveys:

Yama fukami   *Rising, as the mountain*
Mine ni mo tani ni mo   *Peaks and valleys deepen—*

> Koe tatete
> Kyō mo kurenu to
> Higurashi zo naku.

> The twilight sound of the cicada
> Singing of a day
> Already gone by.

Yet a deeper "negative" aspect is the sense of ontological anguish at the universality and inevitability of loss, symbolized by the evaporating dew in #50-J and the withering of plants and trees in #51-J. The "positive" interpretation of transiency is based on the possibilities for renewal and continuity associated with the spring blossoms in #11-J, 20-J, 60-J, 6-C, 8-C, and 9-C, as well as the moral imperative in #7-J, 12-J, 43-J, and 2-C for sustained practice at every moment. Finally, several poems, particularly #14-J, 37-J, and 11-C, go beyond the relativity of celebration and desolation to suggest the nonsubstantive moment of transition without substratum or duration being the metaphysical ground of interpenetrating or overlapping seasonal manifestations. These poems express the original face of primordial time in a way that resembles celebration but reveals a more fundamental affirmation of impermanence "as it is" (*arinomama*).

In his interpretation of such doctrines as *sangai-yuishin* (triple world is mind only), *sokushin-zebutsu* (this very mind is itself the Buddha), and *shinjingakudō* (learning the Way through the mind), Dōgen argues that the universal mind as the ground of phenomenal reality is neither an independent possession nor an entity that views the world as a spectator from a distance. Rather, it is indistinguishable from "walls, fences, tiles, and stones," "mountains, rivers, and earth," or "sun, moon, and sky." The aim of religious experience is to purify and liberate the individual mind to reach an attunement with the holistic, formless truth of concrete reality. Therefore, the perspective of impermanence is determined by the condition of the mind, or the level of authentic subjectivity attained through a realization of the universal mind through observing transiency. The observer must cast off his or her status as spectator and become fully immersed in the unfolding of impermanence. Since the incessancy of change is inalterable, it is incumbent on the mind of the beholder to transform the negative impression on the individual mind into, first, a positive outlook, and, ultimately, a transcendental awareness so that the limited, negative view is converted into a lyrical, holistic standpoint.

The complex and potentially productive role emotions play in the process of awakening the authentic mind is indicated by waka #34-J. The poem highlights the underlying connection between a personal attraction to form and color and the development of a spiritual realization of formlessness by focusing on the word *medekeri* (lit. "love" or "attraction") in the final line, *iro ni medekeri* (lit. "attracted to form"). This phrase, recalling the opening segment of waka #8-J, and identical to the concluding line of #41-J, reinforces Dōgen's emphasis on the role of an emotional attunement to natural beauty. The word *medekeri* (also pronounced *ai*), which also appears in the final sentence of the first paragraph of the Shōbōgenzō "Genjōkōan" fascicle as part of the compound word *aijaku* (sadness) as well as in #54-J where *medeshi* is used, suggests either desirous or compassionate love, depending on the context; both meanings seem implicit here. Like poems #2-J, 19-J, and 29-C, waka #34-J plays off the image of the full moon, a symbol in the Buddhist tradition for the universality of Buddha-nature, and in Court poetry a symbol for longing and consolation:

Ōzora ni	*Contemplating the clear moon*
Kokoro no tsuki o	*Reflecting a mind empty as the open sky—*
Nagamuru mo	*Drawn by its beauty,*
Yami ni mayoite	*I lose myself*
Iro ni medekeri.	*In the shadows it casts.*

This poem contains other terms highly suggestive from a Buddhist standpoint: *iro* (form, the first of the five aggregates that constitute human existence, and the objects of desire); *ōzora* (the "open sky," symbolizing emptiness or nonsubstantiality); and *mayou* (to "lose myself" in the ensnarements of self-imposed ignorance, a concept that is paradoxically identified with enlightenment in Mahayana thought). Through this imagery, the poem asserts the productive interplay between moon and mind, light and dark, and delusion and awakening. To be drawn by the moon for the beauty of its form and color *(iro)* is a self-surpassing experience because it eventually leads to an understanding that the moonlight as the source of illumination mirrors the enlightened mind free of distractions.

In responding to the light, however, even a mind originally or potentially clear *(ōzora)* invariably becomes lost *(mayou)* in the shadows. Yet just as the shadow is a reflection of the true source, interaction with concealed brightness is also edifying. Thus emotions represent both turmoil and the inspiration to awaken from the bondage they cause. The self must continually lose itself in the shadowy world of impermanence to ultimately realize itself liberated from, yet involved in, the unceasing process of continual change. This recalls the doctrine of *ippō-gūjin* (total exertion of a single dharma) expressed in "Genjōkōan," which also uses the moon as a metaphor to disclose the interplay of delusion and enlightenment: "Through the unity of body-mind, forms are seen and voices are heard. Although they are realized intimately, it is not like shadows reflected in a mirror, or the moon in water. When one side is illuminated, the other side is concealed."[11]

In a similar vein, Teika argues that the value of poetic composition is a reflection of the ability of the mind to be actively involved with time and nature, so that "mind and words function harmoniously like the right and left wings of a bird."[12] In the following waka Teika examines the role of the mind:[13]

> *Why blame the moon?*
> *For whether gazing on its beauty*
> *Summons tears,*
> *Or whether it brings consolation,*
> *Depends upon the mind alone.*

Teika and Dōgen concur that the mind can be either mired in

deception or rectified and liberated from distraction and vacillation based on the realization of the mind's capacity to overcome its self-imposed attachments. They see the authentic mind arising from a discipline or cultivation of contemplative awareness, which requires the proper physical posture (just-sitting) and scrupulous concentration, but culminates in a spontaneous or effortless experience. As indicated in the poems of both Dōgen and Teika, the genuine subjectivity of the mind can be understood only in terms of a holistic view of nature symbolized by the moon. It is the experience and description of nature by the authentic subject that seizes on and determines the relativity of the illusion and the truth of impermanent phenomena.

Nature

Dōgen stresses in "Bendōwa" that the instantaneous practice of zazen at once spreads to and is illuminated by the "Buddha activity in which earth, grass, trees, walls, tiles, and pebbles are all involved."[14] Thus zazen engages and completes the realization of each and every phenomenon. The mind, therefore, must heed and identify with the mountains and rivers that embody and reveal the Buddha-nature. This results in the authentication of the mind, or the realization of the universal mind, which experiences the synesthesia of "mountains flowing" or the phantasm of "mountains walking in the sky or on water"; the paradox of the "flowing and non-flowing of the water"; the irony of asking "not whether the observer is enlightened by the mountain but whether the mountain is enlightened by the observer"; and the holistic vision of seeing "a single plum blossom initiating the arrival of spring." The image of blossoms is particularly emphasized in quite a few kanshi verses, including #4-C, 8-C, 9-C, 13-C, 14-C, 27-C, and 33-C. Yet Dōgen is not trying to highlight the attainment of an altered state of consciousness or extraordinary perception; he wants to point to the awareness of nature as it is in its naked or unadorned form. He stresses that beyond the question of whether water does or does not flow is the realization that "water is only thus-itself-the-true-form *{nyoze-jissō}* of water." In his creative rewriting of the traditional saying that the originally empty Buddha takes on form "thus or like *{nyo}* the moon is reflected in water," Dōgen maintains in *Shōbōgenzō* "Tsuki" (The image of the moon), " 'Thus' is [nothing other than] the 'moon in water.' It is water-thus, moon-thus, thus-thus, in-thus. 'Thus' is not 'like' [in the sense of similarity, resemblance, or analogy]. 'Thus' is 'as it is' *(ze)* [or 'nothing other than']."[15] In Chinese kanshi #1-C, Dōgen evokes the directness and immediacy of primordial nature through a deceptively simple description. Any reference to individual response has been eliminated, and the poem expresses a full, unimpeded subjective realization by means of harmony with nature:

> *Every morning, the sun rises in the east;*
> *Every night, the moon sets in the west;*
> *Clouds gathering over the foggy peaks;*
> *Rain passes through the surrounding hills and plains.*

This Chinese verse has an affinity with Japanese poetry, in which nature is generally seen as either a mirror or a model for people. In the first sense, nature reflects human experience and attitudes. Since both humans and nature are bound by the law of incessant change, nature becomes the perfect symbol to represent the way that a human's state of mind is affected by time. For example, the sorrow of lost or unrequited love is seen as resembling fading blossoms, or loneliness is felt like a chilling autumn wind. Yet nature is also depicted as a mystery of transcendental oneness that encompasses and reconciles the transiency that man experiences. In the early stages of poetry, such as Okura's "Lament on instability," nature is seen as enduring and stable in a way that contrasts with, and may either console or mock, man's travails and sense of uncertainty. In the *yūgen* poetry of the period of the *Shinkokinshū* waka collection in the Kamakura era, an experience of full immersion in nature comes to have a healing or soteriological quality when viewed from the contemplative gaze of meditation.

Yūgen poetry is known for its emphasis on pure nature description as the dominant mode of expression, as in the above kanshi verse (#1-C). The depiction of nature is at times so simple and direct that it appears to border on realism, as if striving for a vivid and realistic presentation of intriguing aspects of nature experienced by a distant subject. Yet the intended effect is nearly opposite to realism in that nature depicted in its primordial state is meant to completely mirror the realization of authentic subjectivity with-mind. The aim of *yūgen* poetry is to overcome the gap between poet or subject and poetic object or topic in order to encounter and capture the essentially unified experience of primordial reality. As literary critic Konishi Jin'ichi suggests, "The contemplative expressive approach involves the bracketing of a poet's individual impressions and drawing near to the very essence of the subject. Once the essence has been regained, the poet will recommence grasping forms manifested on a more superficial level of awareness . . . [leaving the reader with] a sense of profound mystery and difficulty."[16] Thus nature is no longer anything external but rather a contemplative field coterminous with the subjective realization of the mind. The poetic description of nature becomes a spontaneous expression of the attainment of subjective realization. For example, the waka

> *About the mountain crest*
> *A brush of cloud floating,*
> *Wild geese fly in files passing*
> *As the moon is hiding behind*
> *A pine tree on the ridge*

carries the headnote "At no time are delusory thoughts to arise in the mind."[17] The subjectivity referred to in the title is deliberately hidden by the depiction of nature in the verse. In fact, there may not appear to be any connection between title and verse (as in

Dōgen's "Original Face"), thereby setting up the paradox that the greater the realization, the less direct or more veiled the expression, so that the latter does not interfere with but allows the complete and unimpeded unfolding of the former.

A famous waka by Teika, which culminates in the image of "descending autumn dusk" *(aki no yūgure),* also used by Saigyō and others, conveys the process of liberating subjectivity through an evocation of a transpersonal atmosphere of supreme desolation *(sabi):*[18]

Miwataseba	*Looking out*
Hana mo monuji mo	*Past where there are*
Nakarikeri	*Cherry blossoms or crimson leaves,*
Ura no tomaya no	*To the grass-thatched huts by the bay*
Aki no yūgure.	*Clustered in the descending autumn dusk.*

The first three lines imply a contemplative flight beyond delimiting horizons that are historical and perceptual in character. The author seeks a path transcending both the poetic tradition, which has relied so heavily on the conventional seasonal images of blossoms and leaves for interpreting transiency, and the ordinary arena of perception, in which the colorful yet fading natural forms seem so irresistibly attractive. The subject thus becomes directly involved in a transcendental experience of nature in its primordial state, unclouded by preconceptions, and the dreary landscape ironically serves as the source of the highest affirmation.

The desolation in Teika's verse may seem at odds with Dōgen's apparent celebration of the anthropomorphized mountains and rivers in waka #6-J, yet both poems are concerned with the attainment of a holistic vision in which the vitality and dynamism of nature may redeem or purify the subject. The structure consists of a negation of the subject through an affirmation of the object of perception. This paradoxical affirmation/negation is based on a realization of the unity of the contemplative field not bound by distinctions. The aim of any attitude is to point beyond personal response to the realm containing and transcending particular perspectives. The question for both Dōgen and the poets is to find an expression that suggests the depths of the experience while using the fewest words so as not to obfuscate the true vision. The expression must be a direct manifestation of the mind's profundity, bypassing false objectification, which reflects an inauthentic personal response to nature. It thereby creates a linguistic field of associations and multiple nuances that manifests the contemplative field of authentic subjectivity. The optimal means of conveying this contemplative stance is a pure description of "water-thusness," "the sun rising in the east," the "autumn dusk descending," or "rice in the bowl, water in the bucket" (as in *Hekiganroku* case 50, cited in Dōgen's kanshi #17-C). These are deceptively simple linguistic vehicles for spontaneously disclosing the ultimate realization.

Illusion

Because of the emphasis on the role of emotions, overcoming inauthenticity can be understood as a process of "illusion surpassing illusion," which is a necessary stage of personal development on the path to "realization beyond realization," according to a passage in the *Shōbōgenzō* "Muchū-setsumu" (Disclosing a dream within a dream) fascicle. This level of understanding indicates that illusion or deception about form is not inherently self-contained and self-defeating but points beyond itself by virtue of being grounded in a previously concealed illuminative awareness of formlessness. In much of Japanese literature expressing *yūgen,* dream is the central metaphor for the transient, formless condition of the phenomenal world such that both "the seeming and the real are true."[19] Dreams may appear to be unreal, but this very unreality, based on nonsubstantiality, provides a hint of the absolute. A waka by Saigyō raises the philosophical issue of the inseparability and reversibility yet the vulnerability of the states of dream and awakening, illusion and reality:[20]

Utsutsu o mo	Because reality
Utsutsu to sarani	Hardly seems real
Oboeneba	Why assume
Yume mo yumeto	That dreams
Nanika omowan.	Are really dreams?

The following Teika verse, generally considered one of the main expressions of *yūgen*, suggests that dream functions as the boundary or horizon separating yet linking the opposites of night and day, past and present, and event and perception:[21]

Haru no yo no	The bridge of dreams
Yume no ukihashi	Floating on the brief spring night
Todae shite	Soon breaks off:
Mine ni wakaruru	Now from the mountaintop a cloud
Yokogumo no sora.	Takes leave into the open sky.

Here the image of "the floating bridge of dreams" (*yume no ukihashi*) highlights the difficulty in determining whether a state is apparent or real as well as the question of whether either condition attains truth; one can be awakened to or from a dream. This image recalls the final chapter of *Genji monogatari,* which is often regarded as a clue to the entire work. Throughout *Genji,* as Ivan Morris indicates, "The idea that the physical world is an illusion, and our lives no more substantial than dew or gossamer, is most often evoked by the imagery of dreams."[22] Also "the open sky" suggests the Buddhist notion of emptiness or formlessness (*kū* or *sora,* also used by Dōgen in waka #10-J, 34-J, and 53-J), which dreams both disclose and conceal.

Waka #36-J (which bears the title "Muchū-setsumu" in some editions of the text) uses a pivot-word and a relational word to amplify the image of dream at once dividing and encompassing illusion and reality:

Moto sue mo	*Like tangled hair,*
Mina itsuwari no	*The circular delusion*
Tsukumo gami	*Of beginning and end,*
Omoi midaruru	*When straightened out,*
Yume o koso toke.	*A dream no longer.*

The pivot-word *tsukumo gami* is an epithet that signifies "ninety-nine hairs," and by extension implies "multitude," "lengthy," or "aging." It could also suggest that the hair of an aging person has grown thin. These implications accentuate the sense of the entanglement pervading "beginning and end" *(moto sue)*—the endless cycle of moral causation—which is a "universal deception" *(mina itsuwari)* that keeps one bound to suffering. When associated with the relational word *toke* (also pronounced *setsu*), which means "to explain or disclose" in the sense of a sermon on the Dharma as well as "to unravel or untie," the image of the hair also suggests that delusion is not irreparable but a temporary condition that can be "straightened out," or a misjudgment that is reversible or reconcilable. Thus the delusion of a world that is as illusory as a dream *(yume)* is clarified as the hair is untangled. That is, the dream is ended by means of the dream itself, and in this process of self-correction it transcends its status as dream or attains a realm wherein dream and awakening merge.

This view opens the door for the apparent unreality or untruth of literary symbols, metaphors, wordplay, and imagery to realize a higher reality. It allows the transcendental quality of lyricism corresponding to *yūgen* to emerge as a crucial stage in the religious quest. Therefore, the level of illusion surpassing illusion converges with and remains inseparable from the level of realization beyond realization: illusion is self-surpassing because it transforms itself into the absolute, and realization is self-surpassing because it must return to a new understanding of the relative. These levels are complementary stages of the continuing process of self-renewing enlightenment. The former as preparatory and the latter as self-perpetuating coincide in the transcendental, all-encompassing moment. The image of dream appears in kanshi #25-C on the Fukakusa retreat. Also #19-C lends a sense of irony to the process of realization by playing off of a traditional image in Chinese poetry of a bird's call, which happens to sound like words of caution to return home. Generally, this image is used in a positive sense, calling wayward souls back to their true source, but Dōgen reverses the meaning from the standpoint of Zen itinerancy and purposeful wandering. He uses the bird's call for another purpose—to show that the itinerant monk doesn't need to be called home, because everywhere is home for him.

> *Treading along in this dreamlike, illusory realm,*
> *Without looking for the traces I may have left;*
> *A cuckoo's song beckons me to return home,*
> *Hearing this, I tilt my head to see*
> *Who has told me to turn back;*
> *But do not ask me where I am going,*
> *As I travel in this limitless world,*
> *Where every step I take is my home.*

Language

In contrast to some approaches in Zen, which regard verbal communication as unnecessary or inherently misleading, Dōgen does not reject or seek to abandon language. Rather, he views language as an inexhaustible reservoir of meaningful ambiguities, all of which are embedded and at times concealed in the words of everyday speech. In *Tenzōkyōkun* Dōgen recounts how he was instructed in the role of language in the practice of the Dharma by an elderly monk he met at the beginning of his trip to China. When Dōgen asked the significance of "words and letters," the monk responded, "One, two, three, four, five . . . Nothing is concealed throughout the entire universe!"[23] This is echoed in "Bendōwa," which asserts, "Let it go and it fills your hand—it is unbound by singularity or multiplicity. Speak and it has already filled your mouth—it is not restricted by lesser or greater."[24] In *Shōbōgenzō* "Sesshin sesshō" (Disclosing mind, disclosing nature) Dōgen stresses the role of "disclosing," "preaching," or "explaining" *(setsu* or *toku)* the Dharma: "The essential function of all Buddhas and patriarchs is disclosing mind, disclosing nature. Their everyday life is disclosing mind, disclosing nature; walls, tiles and stone are disclosing mind, disclosing nature. . . . There is no disclosing without nature, and there is no mind without [the function of] disclosing."[25] Thus all forms of oral and written communication—sutras, epistles, sermons, sayings, poetry, and philosophy—are part of the continual unfolding of the awakened mind. Therefore, Dōgen's view is that language is essential to the transmission of enlightenment. Not only does he deny the view that language is inherently misleading, but he insists that the experience of awakening can and must be symbolically disclosed. Conversely, if the expression of Dharma appears to be incorrect, he suggests that the mistake involves a problematic understanding and not the deficient nature of symbols. Language neither restricts nor conflicts with reality but is an infinite resource for conveying the unlimited meanings of the mind awakened to the multiple aspects of impermanence embodied by nature. Nor is discourse to be understood simply as a discardable "skillful means" *(hōben)* that is used to gain enlightenment and then abandoned once the goal is attained. Discourse is an activity wholly in keeping with true realization, which must be interpreted and discovered continually through language or as an event of expression.

This standpoint seems quite close to the poetic ideal of *yojō,* the aesthetic plenitude of overtones of feeling that is intimately connected with *yūgen. Yojō* implies that the brevity and simplicity of poetic depictions of nature is based on having too much to say or reveal about the mind, so that, writes Chōmei, "many meanings are compressed into a single word, [and] the depths of feeling are exhausted yet not expressed." According to Teika, the "poetic masterpiece must have . . . a profundity and sublimity of mind and creativity of expression allowing an eminently graceful poetic configuration to emerge with an aesthetic plenitude that overflows [or is outside of] words."[26] The notion of a plenitude overflowing words is expressed by Dōgen in two waka (#9-J and 16-J) that rethink the motto "A special transmission outside the teachings *(kyōge betsuden)* / No reliance on words and letters *(furyū monji)*," an apocryphal saying attributed to Bodhidharma and long associated with the Rinzai Zen approach that Dōgen criticizes. Dōgen reads the motto not as an assertion of the priority of silence over speech, as practiced by the followers of Rinzai, but as a sign that verbal expression is a creative resource that reflects and enhances the multifaceted perspectives of realization. In so doing, Dōgen seems to draw inspiration not only from Chinese Zen dialogues and poetry, but from waka techniques that exploit various kinds of wordplay to plumb the depths of language from the standpoint of a spiritualized, aesthetic intentionality. Both waka were delivered during the trip to the Rinzai center in Kamakura. In #9-J, which comments on the first part of the motto, Dōgen critiques the Rinzai approach, which sees enlightenment as outside of the world of conceptual discourse and uses absurd utterances in kōan cases to create an impasse with language and thought that requires a breakthrough to a nonconceptual and nondiscursive understanding. The Rinzai approach fosters subtle dichotomies between language and Dharma, thought and attainment, and thus the relative and the absolute. Dōgen's verse uses several types of wordplay to reinterpret the motto so that it suggests a profound and paradoxical interplay or creative tension between the realms of language and enlightenment:

Kyōge betsuden	*Special transmission outside the teaching*
Araiso no	The Dharma, like an oyster
Nami mo eyosenu	Washed atop a high cliff:
Takayowa ni	Even waves crashing against

> *Kaki mo tsukubeki*   The reefy coast, like words,
> *Nori naraba koso.*   May reach but cannot wash it
>   away.

On first reading, this poem seems to support the conventional Zen view. The "Dharma" *(nori)* resides on a lofty "peak" *(takayowa)*, above and aloof from the controversy and disputation of the world of discourse, symbolized by the "crashing waves" *(nami)* of the "reefy [Echizen] coast" *(araiso)*. Thus the Dharma is located "outside the scriptures" and is not accessible to the written word of the sutras or the recorded sayings. But the full meaning of the waka rests on the use of pivot-words and a relational word whose connotations are so complex and interwoven that they cannot be translated easily. The pivot-words involve the phrase *kaki mo tsukubeki,* which has at least three implications. First, *kaki* can mean "oyster," which implies that the Dharma is not a remote entity above the waves but finds its place beyond the water precisely because of the perpetual motion of the waves. This image plays off the traditional Mahayana analogy of ocean and waves representing universality (absolute) and particularity (relative). Thus the oyster has been cast out of the universal background by the movement of a particular wave but must return to its source for sustenance.

In addition, *kaki* means "writing," suggesting the total phenomenon of language and communication *(kotoba)*, modified by the verb *tsukubeki,* which itself is a pivot-word meaning both "must reach" and "must exhaust." The twofold significance of the phrase "language must reach / must exhaust" heightens the importance of the role of words and accentuates the creative tension between language and Dharma. The Dharma must be expressed. It cannot escape the necessity of discourse, yet the affirmation of the role of language contains the admonition not to use up or exhaust the Dharma through unedifying discussion. The effect of this phrase is enhanced by the relational word *nori,* which means "seaweed" in addition to "Dharma." Seaweed makes an association

figure 5. *Echizen Cliffs*

A view of the glorious rocky coastline along the Japan Sea in Echizen Province; these cliffs probably served as an inspiration for the natural imagery dealing with the issue of language and transcendence in waka #9-J.

with waves and, like *kaki* as oyster, highlights the intimate connection between the conceptual discourse of scripture and the realization of Dharma.

Waka #16-J uses the second part of the motto to stress the priority of language over silence:

Furyū monji	*No reliance on words and letters*
Ii suteshi	Not limited
Sono koto no ha no	By language,
Hoka nareba	It is ceaselessly expressed;
Fude ni mo ato o	So, too, the way of letters
Todome zari keri.	Can display but not exhaust it.

The subject of the poem is not explicitly identified, but the context suggests that it refers to the Dharma. Like the waka just mentioned, this one can be interpreted in at least two ways. One view, based on the title and the opening line, *ii suteshi* (lit. "renounce or cast off speech"), is that the waka asserts the conventional Zen negation of language. A literal rendering that supports this understanding would be "Because the Dharma is outside of language, words are renounced, and the way of letters also leaves no trace on it." In a second, aesthetic interpretation, "nonreliance" is transformed into a positive approach to language because the Dharma is expressed in but is not exhausted by words. Every form of speech and writing is Dharma. Dharma is not limited to any particular aspect of expression, so all possibilities for communication must be explored, and there is no risk of exhausting their source. *Ii suteshi* now means that words are cast off precisely as they are employed; their utility is identical to the act of renouncing them. Similarly, the "way of letters" *(fude)*, a term associated with literary and scriptural texts as well as calligraphy, "leaves no trace" *(ato o todome)*. It does not interfere with or impede but perpetually reveals the multifaceted significance of experience, which, whether enlightened or unenlightened, is a manifestation of the Dharma. *Fude* displays the Dharma without using it up. Silence, in the special *yojō* sense of mysterious depths overflowing words, is advocated by Dōgen not out of an incapacity of expression, but because the Dharma has too many levels of meaning, all of which cannot be held by any particular oral or written discourse. Dōgen's poetic and philosophical works are characterized by a continual effort to express the inexpressible by perfecting imperfectable speech through the creative use of wordplay, neologism, and lyricism, as well as the recasting of traditional expressions.

According to Dōgen's view of the multiple levels of the aesthetics of language, the symbol is real, and reality, in turn, is symbolic. On one level, the symbolism of language—its logic and ambiguities, conventions and deliberate distortions, grammatical structure, and fantastic imagery—is considered real inasmuch as it is a direct emanation of an enlightened perspective of reality. A second level indicates that the phenomena and events, beings and circumstances that constitute the so-called reality of existence are symbolic, and, if truly understood, they express a scriptural discourse on the meanings of impermanence. Dōgen argues that the true nature of language is not limited to words but encompasses the full range of human and natural phenomena. In its daily activity each and every aspect of the universe is a manifestation of impermanence, and as such each and every aspect of the universe is perpetually uttering the inner meaning of the sutras. "When committed to the study of the sutras," Dōgen writes in "Jishōzammai" (Self-realized samadhi), "they truly appear. The sutras are fully manifested throughout the ten directions of the entire universe as mountains, rivers, the whole earth, grass, trees, self, and others."[27] As Dōgen also indicates in the group of five waka on the *Lotus Sutra*, the Mahayana scripture should not be understood merely as a transcribed text. Rather, the changing colors of the mountain peak and the murmuring valley streams (#6-J), the cacophony and echoes of the bustling marketplace (#5-J), even the monkey's cry reverberating in the hills (#4-J)—all resonate with the call of the sutra (#3-J). Furthermore, the sutra is beyond sound; the fleeting image of a horse galloping past the streaming sunlight (#7-J) lyrically evokes the multiple perspectives of impermanence that are the central message of the scripture.

On the third and fundamental level of language unreality is seen as real precisely because it is symbolic. The third level suggests that the apparently unreal or illusory is basically real in that it, too, represents a symbolic manifestation of impermanence. In that light, Dōgen transmutes a number of Zen terms that conventionally indicate the false or fantastic, such as a "dream within a dream" *(muchū-setsumu)*, "painted rice-cake" *(gabyō)*, "flower in the sky" *(kūge)*, or "entangling vines" *(kattō)*, into expressions of transcendental reality that lie beyond the distinctions of truth and untruth. As he writes in *Shōbōgenzō* "Gabyō" (Painted rice-cake), "If there is no painted rice-cake, there is no remedy to satisfy hunger. Furthermore, satisfying hunger, satisfying no-hunger, not satisfying hunger, and not satisfying no-hunger can be neither attained nor expressed without painted hunger."[28] Thus the painting of the rice-cake and hunger, or symbolic expression, is more fulfilling than the tangible cake or physical feeling. The third level goes beyond the assertion of the efficacy and universality of discourse in the first two levels to stress the underlying nondifferentiation whereby reality and unreality merge as symbol. Dōgen also affirms the power of symbolism in citing Ju-ching's verse, "The original face has no birth and death / Spring is in plum blossoms and enters into a painting."[29] According to Dōgen's commentary, spring is not to be identified with the particular image of the flower. Rather, the atmosphere surrounding the entire painting creates and fulfills the experience of spring. According to "Muchū-setsumu," "Having a dream is not a metaphor, but the reality of the Buddha Dharma."[30] Thus any subtle gap or distance is fully eliminated by means of an unimpeded, reciprocal identity. Dreams, painting, and art are not "like" reality: they do not stand for the real or represent it in either a conceptual or a nonconceptual way; they truly and completely manifest its form. There is no "symbol" in the sense of an idea standing for reality, because reality and idea are "thus the moon-reflected-in-water."

Dōgen's standpoint on the complete fusion of polarities in concrete imagery is expressed in waka #61-J, which intertwines the images of moon and dewdrops that are so crucial to Buddhist and poetic expressions of impermanence and nature:

Mujō	*Impermanence*
Yo no naka wa	To what shall
Nani ni tatoen	I liken the world?
Mizudori no	Moonlight, reflected
Hashi furu tsuyu ni	In dewdrops,
Yadoru tsukikage.	Shaken from a crane's bill.

According to this verse, the entire world is fully contained in each and every one of the innumerable dewdrops, each one symbolic of the inexhaustible contents of all impermanent moments. Here the dewdrops no longer suggest illusion in contrast to reality because they are liberated by their reflection of the moon's glow. Conversely, the moon as a symbol of Buddha-nature is not an aloof realm since it is fully merged in the finite and individuated manifestations of the dew. Just as the moon is one with the dewdrops, the poem itself becomes one with the setting it depicts. For Dōgen, all expressions spontaneously and completely realize the authentic mind, which is one with the totality of transient reality. The poem is not a metaphorical pointer to a metaphysical doctrine, but an evocative religio-aesthetic embodiment of the experiential depths of the mind attuned to the impermanence of nature.

Devotional Poems

Several poems express a theme of devotion to the Buddha that is also revealed in the *Shōbōgenzō*. For Dōgen, devotion is not a matter of worshiping an objectified, supernatural entity out of the reach of humanity, but of embracing and venerating the universal truth manifested in all phenomena beyond the dichotomy of self and other. The waka that can be classified as primarily devotional highlight various aspects of religious practice, including the arising of the spiritual quest, penitence and the vow of compassion, and priestly duties and moral exhortations. For example, waka #7-J, 24-J, 29-J, and 43-J counsel disciples on the urgency of the quest for enlightenment and the vigilant exertion needed to overcome suffering. Poem #53-J conveys a sense of ethereal charm that complements the refined elegance of #28-J, for which the moment of devotion is both concrete and celestial, reverberating throughout heaven and earth, which constitute the domain of all Buddhas.

Several of the priestly poems offer an insight into Dōgen's views on agrarian ritual. Waka #46-J deals with the passing of the seasons in terms of the uniformly timed act of changing into summer garments and the consequent opening of the wood monastery doors to hang out a cool bamboo screen. The screen can be interpreted as symbolic of the interaction of the seasons because it creates a separation but also allows for the interpenetration of monastic life and the natural world. The imagery in poems #32-J and 33-J is commonplace, but the verses may provide a rare glimpse of Dōgen's interest in the concerns of farmers through references to spring planting and the celebration of harvest rituals. Dōgen himself is known for remaining uninvolved in missionary or outreach work, instead devoting himself to an austere monasticism. Yet these poems foreshadow the direction taken by Sōtō Zen under the guidance of "second patriarch" Keizan. Although Keizan upheld Dōgen's emphasis on the priority of sustained zazen practice, through his efforts the sect developed into a mass movement that spread throughout the agragrian northern provinces. Sōtō was popular largely because by assimilating popular esoteric rites and prayers with a commitment to causes of social action, it had an eclectic appeal to laypersons.

A pillow-word in waka #44-J helps express the veneration of a Buddha image that remains imperturbable despite its being sullied by a bird's nest and spider's web. This poem apparently refers to an actual incident when Dōgen entered an old and deteriorating mountain temple in his first year in Echizen and was inspired by the calming presence of a statue of the Buddha despite obvious signs of decay (the statue is not explicitly identified in the verse):

Itadaki ni	*Magpie building*
Kasasagi su o ya	*Its nest on his head,*
Tsukururan	*While a spider's web,*
Mayu ni kakareri	*Like tiny crabs,*
Sasagani no ito.	*Covers his eyebrows.*

Here, the pillow-word *sasagani no,* which modifies *ito,* literally means "spider's web," but it also evokes "tiny crabs," thereby stressing the density and persistence of the creatures surrounding the figure, which, although visible signs of deterioration, do not detract from the Buddha's serene and lofty outlook.

A more philosophical approach to the devotional experience is suggested by waka #6-J. This poem, based on a famous Chinese verse cited in the *Shōbōgenzō* "Keisei-sanshoku" (Sounds of valleys, colors of mountains) fascicle, stresses the identity of mountains-rivers with the body and voice of Buddha. It extends the doctrine of the "true form of all dharmas" *(shohō jissō)* by concluding that not only does the Buddha preach to all things, but all things as they are in themselves are preaching the Dharma and enlightening humans:

Mine no iro	*Colors of the mountains,*
Tani no hibiki mo	*Streams in the valleys;*
Mina nagara	*One in all, all in one,*
Waga Shakamuni no	*The voice and body of*
Koe to sugata to.	*Our Sakyamuni Buddha.*

This waka also recalls the view expressed in *Shōbōgenzō* "Sansuikyō" (Mountains and rivers sutras) that each and every aspect of nature is the continuous preaching of the sutras. The key to the poem is *waga* (our), which indicates the inseparability and intimate rapport

figure 6. *Eiheiji River*

A view of a bridge over the waters streaming down the mountain location of Eiheiji, which inspired waka #6-J and other poems on the beauty of nature and the changing of the seasons.

of humans and Buddha, as well as the unity of nature personified and of humans identified with the entire environment. Here *iro* (colors), which in early Buddhism implies the forms of attachment, has a positive connotation pointing to the concrete manifestations of universal emptiness. The final phrase, *koe to sugata to* (voice and body), supports the concluding line of waka #3-J, which suggests an identity of "voice and heart" *(koe to kokoro to)* and the *Lotus Sutra*.

Similarly, in kanshi #13-C Buddha is identified with nature personified. The following Chinese verse, #35-C, offers a glimpse of the Zen master in a repentant mood as he strives to renew perpetually his enlightenment experience:

> *In a thatched hut in this deep mountain recess,*
> *Ceaselessly practicing meditation and contemplation,*
> *Yet dust keeps gathering even on this high peak of virtue,*
> *As I long to attain supranormal powers* [jinzū] *as a follower of*
> *the Tathagata.*

The final line may indicate a potential equality of the aspirant and the ultimate, as this translation suggests, or it may be interpreted as conveying an appeal to the saving power of Buddha if the line is rendered as follows: "My plea is to be saved by the supranormal powers of the Tathagata."

Personal Poems

The personal poems, the final category in this analysis of themes in Dōgen's collections, reveal key aspects of Dōgen's feelings, including his sense of uncertainty, frustration, or ambivalence about his relation to Kyoto as well as the poetic tradition. Several of the devotional poems can also be considered autobiographical in that they disclose the awakening of Dōgen's spiritual impulse or his resolve to seek the Buddhist Way. Waka #23-J refers to the initial occasion of religious aspiration through a conventional wordplay on *afumi*, which literally means "I meet" and also refers to the "hollyhock festival" *(aoi matsuri)*, an annual Shinto parade in Kyoto in early summer, known as a time for renewing old acquaintances. The implication on one level is that out of the confusion of a chance meeting when one has traveled (suggested by *gusa*; lit. "grass") for another reason (Shinto ritual), a new sense of purpose and direction (pursuit of Dharma) happens to arise. The significance in terms of Dōgen's life may be that out of the context and influence of his Kyoto upbringing, he chose a path that demanded a renunciation of that very background.

Several other poems represent Dōgen's reflections on feelings either at a critical point in his life and spiritual path or in relation to his work and its acceptance. Waka #1-J and 2-J on the final Kyoto journey, as well as #8-J on the first Echizen snowfall, bear headnotes that announce their topics. In addition to these, #40-J on his hectic activity and travels between Kippōji and other temples and #44-J on confronting a Buddha image with a dignified facade despite the otherwise dilapidated condition of the unused temple in the remote provinces seem to suggest actual events that took place shortly after Dōgen's move from the Kyoto region. Waka #37-J expresses his mixed emotions concerning Echizen and Kyoto, while #12-J, 19-J, and 28-C comment on Dōgen's resolve during the taxing Kamakura trip, despite feelings of vulnerability and uneasiness, to face a potentially unfriendly audience of sectarian opponents. Also #26-J suggests disdain for those who would give a facile interpretation to his works.

Aristocratic Background

Dōgen's drive toward religious awakening was inspired, according to traditional sources, by a combination of an aristocratic birthright and the tragic loss of his parents in early childhood, although modern scholars have raised questions about the historicity of these events. In waka #31-J Dōgen reveals his profound sense of loss about the untimely death of his parents, and his deep and continuing sense of grief about their death:

Mutsu no michi	*My companions*
Ochikochi mayou	*Trekking*
Tomogara wa	*The six realms—*
Waga chichi zo kashi	*I recognize my father!*
Waga haha zo kashi.	*There is my mother!*

The poem suggests that Dōgen never fully overcame the suffering the loss of his parents caused him. Instead, he attempted to integrate an attunement to sorrow with the quest for spiritual release.

China

After Dōgen spent ten years experimenting with different forms of Buddhism in Japan in the Kyoto area, the next stage of his renunciation of the secular life in the capital was his journey to China in 1223. Dōgen had been studying Tendai, Shingon, and Zen Buddhism at Kenninji Temple since 1217 after several years of wandering on Mt. Hiei. Kenninji, the first Japanese temple to give instruction in Zen, was founded by Eisai, who introduced an eclectic form of Rinzai Zen to Japan based on his travels to China. On his overseas pilgrimage, Dōgen accompanied Myōzen, Eisai's foremost disciple, who died during the journey. Dōgen undertook the journey because of his fundamental doubt concerning the conceptual veracity and religious efficacy of the Tendai doctrine of original enlightenment. In *Shōbōgenzō zuimonki* Dōgen makes it clear that part of his motive for traveling to China was a disdain for the moral laxity and philosophical ineptitude of some of the Japanese priests whom he had come to regard "as so much dirt and broken tile." In other writings Dōgen is also critical of many of the Chinese Zen masters and temples he encountered before his apprenticeship to Ju-ching. Although he does not refer to literature as a factor in his criticism at this period, it might be assumed that he considered the "art for art's sake" attitude pervading Buddhist practice in both China and Japan to be a pernicious influence detracting from the authentic Dharma.

Yet during his stay in China Dōgen was drawn to the teachings of Hung-chih and Ju-ching, both of whom were noted for their Zen poetry. In his verses written in China we find Dōgen consoling a layman on the death of his son in #21-C and refuting the supernatural religiosity associated with the pilgrimage site at Mt. Potolaka, considered the earthly abode of the bodhisattva Kannon, in #22-C. In his Chinese poems there are also the seeds of what was to become the dominant creative feature of Dōgen's philosophy: his willingness to revise and rewrite the sayings of earlier texts and patriarchs, including his own mentor, as in the poems on the moon in #29-C; on the ringing of the bell in #41-C, which recalls the *Shōbōgenzō* "Inmo" (Suchness) fascicle; and in the death verse, #47-C.

Fukakusa

On returning home from China, Dōgen, eager to establish the Chinese style of Zen monasticism in Japan, at first stayed at Kenninji for three years and wrote *Fukanzazengi,* his manifesto on the priority of zazen-only practice. Because of the social and political problems plaguing Kyoto, as well as the decline of monastic standards at Kenninji and disputes over doctrine there, Dōgen moved to Fukakusa in 1230, where be stayed for over a dozen years before taking up residence in Echizen. He first occupied the abandoned temple An'yōin, where he wrote "Bendōwa," which remains the leading introduction to his thought. In 1233 he took over a former Pure Land temple of the Fujiwara clan, Kannon dori-in, and composed "Genjōkōan," the opening and in many ways the most innovative fascicle of the *Shōbōgenzō,* which uses the image of the unmarked pathways of birds and fish as a metaphor for traceless enlightenment (recalling waka #15-J). Three years later, Dōgen built a new monks hall and reopened the temple as Kōshōji, the first independent Zen center in Japan. This work inspired the writing of his collection of Chinese poems on ninety kōans written in the style known as *juko* (see #38-C–46-C in Chapter Four). *Juko* are four-line verses, the form used in early Buddhist poetry (Skt. *gâtha*) and commonly used by Chinese masters who compiled kōan collections. But Dōgen's use of this style for commenting on paradigmatic dialogues proved to be an experiment that he ultimately abandoned in favor of the *Shōbōgenzō*'s Japanese prose style of explicating kōan cases. The creative peak of Dōgen's career also began at Kōshōji as he completed the majority of the most philosophically compelling *Shōbōgenzō* fascicles, including "'Busshō," "Uji," and "Zenki" (Total dynamism). Many of the *Shōbōgenzō* fascicles that are richest in poetic feeling and natural imagery were written during the Fukakusa period, including "Sansuikyō" and "Keisei-sanshoku," which identify the Buddha-nature with the changing colors of mountains and the murmuring or torrential sounds of valley streams.

In Dōgen's verse during this period a mixed picture emerges as to the relation of Buddhism and literature, reflecting the general sense of ambivalence in Dōgen's stance. Dōgen's departure from Kyoto was based on a desire to establish the independence and integrity of his brand of religious practice. On the one hand, the move was another reaction to the secular distractions of Court-influenced Buddhism, probably involving art. But the site of Fukakusa (lit. "deep grass") is significant from an aesthetic standpoint. The village is celebrated in Court poetry as an idyllic retreat secluded from the tribulations of the capital. Dōgen's attitude there, reflected in one of his better-known Chinese poems, #25-C, may represent a deepening of his aesthetic attunement to nature, rather than a rejection of art, or a deepening of his identification with the religio-aesthetic sense of loneliness, which at once implies a criticism of Kyoto culture and an enhancement of the aesthetic outlook associated with the capital:

> Drifting pitifully in the whirlwind of birth and death,
> As if wandering in a dream [muchū],
> In the midst of illusion I awaken to the true path;
> There is one more matter I must not neglect,
> But I need not bother now,
> As I listen to the sound of the evening rain
> Falling on the roof of my temple retreat
> In the deep grass of Fukakusa.

This verse, one of a series of six kanshi on the "time of my retreat," suggests an atmosphere of profound mystery or *yūgen* as the loneliness of a rainy night is transformed into a moment of religio-aesthetic solitude transcending the deceptions of ignorance and attachment and the polarity of life and death. This contemplative moment, which goes beyond the need to save other beings ("one more matter"), also recalls the raindrop sound leading to enlightenment in #56-J and 31-C, as well as the emphasis on a single experience of nature triggering *satori* in three poems dealing with Ling-yun's viewing the peach blossoms, #11-J, 4-C, and 44-C. Also the sequence of "Five poems on the *Lotus Sutra*" accentuates the development of Dōgen's aesthetic perspective during the Fukakusa period. This series on the Mahayana sutra, which Dōgen prizes most highly, affirms the identity of scripture and nature, recalling the *Shōbōgenzō* fascicles cited previously.

Echizen

Unfortunately, Dōgen's success at Kōshōji engendered jealousy and hostility among the rival, more established Buddhist sects, particularly the still dominant Tendai sect, and he left for Echizen in his final and most important renunciation of Kyoto-based religion and society. Dōgen's removal to Echizen represented a continuation of the Fukakusa longing for freedom from sectarian disputes and secular distractions, and it also fulfilled Ju-ching's

figure 7. *Fukakusa Retreat*

A few years after returning from China in 1227, Dōgen stayed in a small, older temple in the town of Fukakusa just outside of Kyoto, celebrated in Court poetry because the name literally means "deep grass." This period inspired a number of his Chinese poems, especially #25-C on the sound of the rain falling on the temple roof, as shown in a drawing from a series of illustrations done in the Tokugawa era of key events in Dōgen's biography.

injunction that Dōgen remain aloof from political and social pressures even at the risk of having only a few serious disciples. One significant aspect of the study of Dōgen's poetry involves the dating of its composition in relation to his other works, especially the *Shōbōgenzō*. Dōgen moved to Echizen in the summer of 1243 and stayed for a year at Kippōji Temple, while also preaching at Yamashibūdera Temple, until the summer of 1244, when he opened Daibutsuji Temple (the name was changed to Eiheiji in 1246). The interim year at Kippōji was marked by a continuation of his high Fukakusa output of *Shōbōgenzō* fascicles, including "Sesshin sesshō," "Sangai yuishin" (Triple world is mind only), "Kūge" (Flowers of emptiness), and "Shohō jissō" (True form of all Dharmas) among many others. After settling in at Eiheiji, Dōgen's writing for the *Shōbōgenzō* quickly diminished, and the fascicles completed there tended to focus on explicitly monastic matters rather than broader philosophical themes. During this time, however, his composition of poetry, especially Chinese verses, significantly increased, so that poetic expression became a major feature of the Echizen period. Thus Dōgen ironically found a role for poetry just when he was furthest removed from Kyoto and most dedicated to puritanical monasticism. An interesting combination of poetic and monastic themes can be found in the final series of the kanshi collection called the "twenty-four hours," which contains twelve verses (#36-C and 37-C are examples) on two-hour cycles in the monk's daily life, involving meals, meditation, chores, and sleeping (and dreaming).

Both the Japanese and the Chinese verses are useful in understanding Dōgen's feelings during this culminating segment of his spiritual work. Since both the autobiographical reflections and the biographical accounts of the Echizen period are sketchy or scarce, the poetry offers an unusual glimpse into the author's attitudes at this exhilarating time. Several waka, including #8-J, 44-J, and 40-J, convey Dōgen's initial impressions in Echizen and Eiheiji. The latter verse is noteworthy for its use of wordplay and seasonal imagery to convey Dōgen's ambivalence about his distance from Kyoto, grounded in a sensitivity to the fleeting nature of time:

> Azusa yumi
> Haru kure-hatsuru
> Kyō no hi o
> Hikitodometsutsu
> Ochikochi yaran.
>
> Dispersed, as today's
> Spring light fades,
> Yet stays held taut,
> Like a catalpa bow:
> My travels are never ending.

Ochikochi is a pivot-word that literally means "hither and thither," dramatizing the struggle between Dōgen's almost frantic pace and the fading of the spring light. It also suggests "regret" *(oshimu)* for the loss of time and, perhaps, for his absence from the Kyoto/Fukakusa area.

There is much debate about why Dōgen moved to Echizen, with some theorists speculating that he was driven away by conflicts with jealous sects, and others suggesting that he chose an area from which many of his new supporters hailed. It is clear that a central motivation for Dōgen's selection of Echizen was the example provided by early Chinese Zen masters, of whom he considered Ju-ching a rare embodiment. Dōgen's predecessors were known for their uncompromising commitment to isolating their pursuit of Buddhism from all worldly concerns. As Hee-Jin Kim notes of Eiheiji, "Dōgen at last revitalized his long-cherished dream: the establishment of an ideal monastic community as envisioned by Pai-chang Huai-hai (749–814) in the bosom of mountains and waters."[31] Another source of inspiration for Dōgen's embracing the mountains and waters *(sansui)* of remote Echizen as his religious "center of the world" *(axis mundi),* however, seems to be the Japanese religio-aesthetic practice of setting up a permanent grass-thatched hut or hermitage *(sōan)* to serve as a mountain retreat *(yamazato).* The largest section of Dōgen's waka collection, for example, contains over thirty-three verses titled "Impromptu hermitage poems" *(Sōan no gūei),* many of which celebrate the natural beauty and seasonal changes of Echizen. Also a majority of Dōgen's Chinese verses are from the Echizen period, such as the series on the "snow" and the "mountain retreat," which deal with the theme of spiritual purification through mountain solitude (see #30-C–35-C).

An emphasis on mountains and rivers as the true locale of the enlightenment experience can also be found in Kūkai and Saichō, the respective founders of the Japanese Shingon and Tendai sects. According to Ienaga Saburō's analysis, the *yamazato* ideal that surfaced in the late Heian/early Kamakura periods is based on the fundamentally Japanese view of nature as a mirror and model for humans:[32]

> The ideal of the *yamazato* life as a retreat in the mountains, even though shaped in part by Chinese and Buddhist motifs and concepts, is ultimately rooted in the ancient Japanese love of nature; the charm of the *yamazato* depends really upon the amenability of Japanese to be captivated by nature's beauty . . . that is expressed through the image of the mountain retreat which makes nature to be soteric *(kyūsai).*

Ienaga indicates that the value of the grass hut for writers/priests such as Saigyō and Chōmei is not merely that it is located far from the contaminations of civilization and allows for a communion with nature, which would imply a subtle gap between humans and their surroundings. Nor does it represent a form of nature-worship, or of viewing the mountains as sacred in contrast to the profane, as is typical in folk religion. Rather, as for Thoreau in America centuries later, the mountain hermitage, deliberately built to highlight the permeability and porousness of artificial constructions, teaches a daily lesson about impermanence involving the integration of all elements in nature flowing in unison with the physical and spiritual aspects of human existence. Such a seamless and holistic or fundamentally nonsubstantive experience of nature is the basis of religious fulfillment for many writers.

Ienaga does not cite Dōgen as an example of the *yamazato* experience, and there are numerous differences between the Zen master's approach to the mountains and that of the reclusive writers. The recluses tend to embrace the feeling of loneliness or desolation *(sabi)* by internalizing their observation of the frailty of nature and highlighting the qualitative differences between civilization and the mountain setting. Chōmei's account of his decision for renunciation reflects a belief in the Pure Land notion of the Age of Decline *(mappō)*, which Dōgen specifically refutes with the notion of the Age of the True Law *(shōbō)*. Dōgen's view of mountains stresses the perpetual renewal of nature, as represented by the early spring plum blossoms *(baige)*. He writes, "When the old plum tree spontaneously comes into bloom, the flowering of the entire world emerges. The moment that the flowering of the entire world is manifested is itself the arrival of spring."[33] In addition, Dōgen affirms nature as the locus for the continual teaching of the Dharma by both sentient and insentient (mountains, rivers, and so forth) beings, as in Chinese verse #40-C.

Dōgen's verse on the Fukakusa rain (#25-C) cited previously can be interpreted in light of the *yamazato* ideal. The hermitage experience he describes is a simple but vividly concrete example of soteriological serenity found through solitude, by letting the fragility and instability of the natural environment overwhelm the mind and block out all distractions. The poem is based on a thoroughgoing contemplative unity with the sound of the rain in and of itself, without reference to an individual subject. Other poems suggest that the mountain retreat is a key to his realization of the Dharma, such as kanshi #32-C:

> *Transmitting to the east the way the ancestors brought from the west,*
> *My daily activities illuminated by the moon and shadowed by the clouds,*
> *Because I revere the ancient way of the patriarchs,*
> *The secular dust of worldly customs does not reach*

> Where I remain secluded in my grass-thatched hut,
> On a snowy evening deep in the mountain recesses.

Note the contrast with #35-C, which suggests that the dusty world continues to intrude on the mountain retreat.

In waka #13-J Dōgen identifies the inner recesses of mountain pathways with Buddhist enlightenment through a wordplay connecting the isolated retreat or village (*sato*) and sudden awakening (*satori*). The poem also combines the conventional techniques of the pivot-word and the relational word in conjunction with the theme of travel to comment on its title, "True seeing received at birth." This headnote, taken from a passage of the *Lotus Sutra* (chapter 19), concerns the primordial Buddha-nature or original face, which in this verse is attained through a journey into the mountains. In addition, the imagery of the poem recalls the parable from the same scripture from the sutra (chapter 4) of the prodigal son who has returned home, a parable symbolizing an awakening to the originality and universality of the Buddha-nature that is only seemingly lost and then rediscovered:

Fubo shoshō no manako   *True seeing received at birth*

Tazune iru	Seeking the Way
Miyama no oku no	Amid the deepest mountain paths,
Sato nareba	The retreat I find
Moto sumi nareshi	None other than
Miyako nari keri.	My *primordial home:* satori!

Here the fulfillment of the travel motif is expressed in that the place found at the end of the journey is none other than the initial home, thus suggesting a unity of original and acquired enlightenment. The pivot-word *miyako* literally means "capital," or, specifically, "Kyoto," and implies the comfort and satisfaction of one's true home. The authentic home is located far from the actual Kyoto, yet it is no different than the essential nature of the capital. When the syllables are pronounced separately as *mi ya ko*, however, the phrase signifies "body and child." This wordplay elaborates on the title by implying that genuine insight received as a potentiality at birth is not realized until the body develops. So the progression does not lead beyond or out of but is precisely a return to the initial home. *Mi* (body) also associates with *miyama* or "deep mountains," indicating that the mountains have become the new body, which is fundamentally the same as the original home despite the length of the journey. Finally, *sato* as "home" or "village" evokes a spontaneous awakening *(satori)* to the knowledge of ways already present, though not previously attained, of the inseparability of the potentiality and the actuality of enlightenment.

Several of Dōgen's waka celebrate the beauty marked by the transiency of the Echizen seasons, including #5-J, 27-J, 37-J, 38-J, 39-J, 52-J, 54-J, and 60-J, which deal with the particular and distinctive features of each season as well as the overlapping and cyclical quality of the four seasons. Other poems use Echizen imagery as a backdrop for making a philosophical point or for devotional expression, as in the cliffs symbolizing language in #9-J, the mountain paths representing enlightenment in #13-J, and the hut and fields providing a basis for worship in #21-J and 32-J. A key example of the use of Echizen imagery appears in #38-J, which conveys a sense of longing for the multiple aspects of Kyoto (here, again, *miyako* means both the literal capital and one's symbolic "home"), along with the crisis of alienation this feeling generates:

> *Miyako ni wa* All last night and
> *Momiji shinuran* This morning still,
> *Okuyama no* Snow falling in the deepest
>   mountains;
>
> *Koyoi mo kesa mo* Ah, to see the autumn leaves
> *Arare furi keri.* Scattering in my home.

This poem suggests Dōgen's ambivalent attitude toward literature and aesthetics in several ways. On a literal level, the early Echizen snow is a reminder that Kyoto is still enjoying a gentler and more graceful seasonal transition of autumn leaves; many of the kanshi verses record this same shock at the new climate. There is something pleasant and appealing about Kyoto in comparison with the extreme and now barren mountain climate.

The famous kanshi #15-C, which accompanies a moon-viewing *(tsukimi)* self-portrait completed in 1249, turns this landscape into a symbol for enlightenment. Yet the snows must also soon come to the capital, and the feelings of nostalgia perhaps also heighten the appreciation of Echizen. On a symbolic level, the waka indicates that the attraction of Kyoto and all that it represents is never fully abandoned, although Dōgen cannot return there. A choice between Echizen and Kyoto must be and, of course, is made despite the mixed feelings. Dōgen's ambivalence about returning to Kyoto, vividly portrayed in waka #2-J, may parallel the ambivalent feelings of solitude and loneliness, and the independence and longing that Ienaga argues are central to the grass-hut literary motif, in which the "*yamazato* hermit . . . may even wistfully dream of the happy bustle of city life. But of course a return to the city and its complexities could only make things worse."[34]

Seen in light of Dōgen's life and writings, however, waka #38-J points beyond feelings of ambiguity, uncertainty, or tension. At the basis of Dōgen's apparent ambivalence about geographical and cultural landscapes is a profound philosophical paradox underlying the relationship between religion and aesthetics, transcendence and emotion, and absolute realization and concrete or relative experience. Attaining enlightenment involves missing and longing for aesthetic experience and expression. But lyricism need not be excluded from the spiritual life if the appropriate paradoxical perspective about the interconnectedness of aesthetics and religion is maintained.

Kamakura and Death

Dōgen's creative ambivalence is also expressed in kanshi #28-C, written near the end of his trip to Kamakura in 1248, after he had been away from Eiheiji for nearly eight months. He writes "on hearing an early spring thunderstorm":

> *For six months I've been taking my rice at the home of a layman,*
> *Feeling like the blossoms of an old plum tree covered by the snow and frost,*
> *Exhilarated in hearing the first sound of thunder crackling across the sky—*
> *The five red petals of spring peach blossoms will soon be brightening the capital.*

The "layman" referred to in the first line is actually his patron, Hatano. Dōgen clearly misses the life of ritual purity at Eiheiji yet longs for a return to the capital (it is ambiguous whether "capital" refers to Kyoto or to the temporary capital in Kamakura).

Dōgen is not interested in going as far as the *yamazato* writers in isolating himself in a withered hermitage away from all companionship and convention. His concern is the establishment of a viable monastic community based on a philosophical understanding of the inseparability of self and nature, spontaneity and continuity, and the independent spirit and the interdependence of all phenomena. It is important to recognize that Dōgen's primary activity during the Echizen period was the delivery of sermons collected in the first seven volumes of the *Eihei kōroku,* the main text of his last ten years and perhaps a close second to the *Shōbōgenzō* in overall importance and for understanding his life and thought. These sermons, known as *jōdō* (lit. "entering the Dharma Hall and ascending the high seat on the platform"), were delivered according to a regimented schedule, following the style of Chinese masters. These include many verse commentaries on kōans, sutra passages, and other anecdotes (as in #1-C–14-C). The general pattern was to present a short prose statement, allow for a pause during which there was probably time for discussion and debate, and then offer the poem, which probably had little direct, logical connection to the main sermon but was an indirect, subjective, or intuitive commentary on it. In some cases the poem was the entire sermon, as in #12-C on the meditation posture:

> *My nose is in line with my navel,*
> *My ears are on the same plane as my shoulders.*

Finally, Dōgen's death verse *(yuige)* in Chinese, #47-C, was composed, according to traditional sources, as were most death verses of the Zen masters, as he awaited his demise while sitting in the zazen position. He rewrites his mentor Ju-ching's poem, which focuses on "Yellow Springs" that in popular culture usually refers to hell but is used as an image in Zen writings to suggest *nirvana*:

> *For sixty-six years*
> *Committing terrible sins against heaven,*
> *Now leaping beyond,*
> *While still alive, plunging into the Yellow Springs;*
> *Amazing! I used to believe that*
> *Life and death were unrelated.*

Although in some cases Dōgen does show a penitent attitude, here, unlike in his mentor's confession, he deletes any reference to "sin" and displays confidence and bravado mixed with irony or uncertainty about the final outcome:

> *For fifty-four years*
> *Following the way of heaven;*
> *Now leaping beyond,*
> *Shattering every barrier,*
> *Amazing! To cast off all attachments,*
> *While still alive, plunging into the Yellow Springs.*

PART II

TRANSLATIONS OF THE JAPANESE AND CHINESE COLLECTIONS

CHAPTER THREE

A Small Boat Drifting: The Japanese Poetry Collection

THIS CHAPTER contains a complete translation of Dōgen's collection of thirty-one-syllable waka, or Japanese verses. The text is based on several sources, which are indicated in Appendix A. The collection has traditionally been known as "Sanshōdōei" (Verses on the Way from Sanshō Peak [the original name of the mountain location of Eiheiji, the Temple of Eternal Peace]). But this title was first used several centuries after the collection was published, so most scholars prefer to refer to the collection as simply "Dōgen waka-shū" (Dōgen's waka collection). The collection initially appeared as part of the main biography of Dōgen, the *Kenzeiki*, published in 1472, which reports that it was constructed by a Sōtō temple abbot in 1420. The earliest manuscripts of the *Kenzeiki* are from the sixteenth century, which means that there is a gap of more than three hundred years between the time of Dōgen and his disciple-editors and the extant versions of the waka collection. During the Tokugawa-era revival of Sōtō sect scholarship, there were additional manuscripts and commentaries

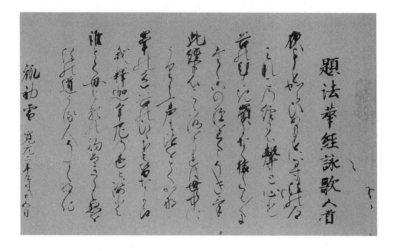

figure 8. *Waka Calligraphy*

The opening passages of Dōgen's waka collection in a late medieval version of the text from Dōgen Zenji Zenshū, volume VII; note the flowing Japanese calligraphic style contrasted with Dōgen's *Fukanzazengi* calligraphy in Chapter Two.

on the text, especially by Menzan Zuihō, some of which are at odds on different points with the older manuscripts.

Because there are numerous discrepancies among the various versions of the poetry text, there are two main issues to be considered. First, modern scholars have verified the authenticity of fifty-three of the sixty-three waka; the other ten are questionable, but they are included in the main Japanese editions of Dōgen's works. The status of the ten additional or supplementary poems is discussed more fully below. The second issue is more complicated. It appears that Menzan's version of the *Kenzeiki* biography containing the poetry, which was considered the standard edition until Dōgen scholarship advanced considerably in the postwar period, contained inaccurate emendations to the text. Some of these are merely inconsistencies, but others are apparently part of a campaign to idealize Dōgen's biography. For instance, Menzan exaggerated the status of Dōgen's aristocratic birth and upbringing to place Dōgen closer to the center of Court society in order to dramatize his eventual Buddhist renunciation of secularized Kyoto. The effect of such a portrayal is to reinforce a sense of distance between Dōgen and the world of literature. But as the picture of Dōgen's choices painted by Menzan undergoes revision through contemporary studies, the analysis of Dōgen's view of poetry has also changed, even though the full story of his life may remain vague and elusive to modern historians.

In the case of the waka collection, Menzan's text contains several inaccuracies. Some of the poems are slightly altered, and in a couple of cases this greatly affects the meaning of the verse. The waka form, deliberately ambiguous owing to its reliance on wordplay and conceits for literary effect, is particularly susceptible to both disparities of interpretation and controversies concerning textual variations. Different understandings of the meaning of one word or even a single syllable, perhaps chosen by the author precisely to suggest multiple nuances, can lead to significantly different interpretations of an entire poem. The alternative renderings of "Original Face," as discussed in Chapter One, are not based on a dispute about what the words actually are, just about the interpretation. But in the following example of a relatively straightforward, unambiguous poem, there is an important discrepancy between Menzan's rendering and the earlier versions of the waka text, and the discrepancy does change the meaning of the verse. This is one of a group of five waka on the *Lotus Sutra* alluding to a Zen anecdote in which a monk claims to have paradoxically attained enlightenment upon hearing a merchant hawking his wares at the market. This verse recalls the image in the Ten Oxherding Pictures, in which the boy, after having captured and tamed the ox and then reverted to a state of absolute nothingness, emerges to return to ordinary reality and enters the marketplace. Here is the version in Menzan's text:

> *Kono kyō no*   Attaining the heart
> *Kokoro o ureba*   Of the sutra,
> *Yo no naka ni*   The sounds of the
> *Urikau koe mo*   Bustling marketplace
> *Nori o toku keri.*   Preach the Dharma.

This version suggests a strong affirmation of the sounds of the marketplace as being identical to the Dharma from the standpoint of one who has attained the heart or inner meaning of the Mahayana scripture. As in the Ten Oxherding Pictures, the implication is that everyday life is ultimately indistinguishable from enlightenment; all apparent oppositions are harmoniously reconciled.

While this meaning certainly seems compatible with Dōgen's nondualistic philosophy, the version in the earlier *Kenzeiki* manuscripts contains a subtle but important difference as *uru wa* (to attain) is substituted for *ureba* ("because you attain") in line 2, and, more important, *kawa* (an ironic questioning) replaces *keri* (a mildly exclamatory remark) in the final line:

> *Kono kyō no*   Attaining the heart
> *Kokoro o uru wa*   Of the sutra,

> *Yo no naka ni* Are not even the sounds
> *Urikau koe mo* Of the bustling marketplace
> *Nori o toku kawa.* The preaching of the Dharma?

This version expresses a sense of irony *(hango)* rather than a direct affirmation, thereby challenging instead of asserting the identification of commerce with spirituality. Also the association between the terms *uru* (to buy) and *urikau* (marketplace, lit. "buying and selling") leaves the reader to wonder whether the chaos of materialism and the transcendental release of the Dharma can be so easily equated. At least one is warned not to misinterpret the meaning of nonduality from a facile perspective. From the standpoint of the second version, the first version appears one-sided and simplistic, overlooking the guiding principle of the Buddhist middle way standing between and beyond assertion and denial. The second version does seem to allow the equality of marketplace and Dharma, which is not directly negated, but an aesthetic doubt is deliberately left hanging.

The same sort of issue applies to #17-J, for which Menzan's version substitutes *shizumu* (sinking down) in the last line for *shiranami* (white waves), thereby losing the meaning of vacillation as the white gull blends in with the color of the waves. A related issue appears in #47-J if *mi* in the last line is read as the *kanji* "to see" rather than "body," which the translation here suggests, so that the meaning of the unity and insubstantiality of the body-mind is obscured.

The following translations are presented in the way that the waka collection is usually presented in Japanese editions, divided into six main subsections based on common styles or dates of composition.

Group 1 "The Final Journey" (#1-J–2-J)

This group includes the first two poems in the collection in the

Kenzeiki version of the text written during Dōgen's final journey to Kyoto, begun on the eighth month, fifth day of 1253, when he was persuaded by patron Hatano Yoshishige to return to the capital for medical treatment after ten years' absence. Dōgen reached Kyoto, but died on the twenty-eighth day of that month in the home of a lay disciple while in the zazen posture, according to traditional biographies. Waka #1-J was composed while crossing Kinobe Pass halfway between Eiheiji and Kyoto, and #2-J was composed at the time of the harvest moon. These poems play off the conventional poetic themes of travel and contemplation of the moon to evoke Dōgen's sense of longing and regret, and his anticipation and exhilaration, concerning Kyoto, as well as his imminent encounter with death. For Dōgen, Kyoto represents not only his birthplace, aristocratic heritage, and literary upbringing but also the capital and repository of Japanese culture and the Buddhist hierarchical establishment, which he renounced for the mountain solitude and natural purity of Eiheiji Temple. Dōgen's Chinese death verse is #47-C in Chapter Four.

1-J

Go-jōraku no sono hi go—	The {final} journey to
shōka kore ari shō ni iwaku	Kyoto
Kusa no ha ni	Like a blade of grass,
Kadodeseru mi no	My frail body
Kinobe yama	Treading the path to Kyoto,
Kumo ni oka aru	Seeming to wander
Kokochi koso sure.	Amid the cloudy mist on Kinobe Pass.[1]

2-J

Gyo-nyūmetsu no toshi	On the eighth month/fifteenth
hachigatsu jūgoya	day {harvest} moon in the year
go-eika ni iwaku	of Dōgen's death[2]

Mata minto	Just when my longing to see
Omoishi toki no	The moon over Kyoto
Aki dani mo	One last time grows deepest,
Koyoi no tsuki ni	The image I behold this autumn night
Nerare yawa suru	Leaves me sleepless for its beauty.

Group 2 "Five Poems on the Lotus Sutra" *(#3-J–7-J)*

This group contains five waka inspired by contemplation of the *Lotus Sutra* (Jap. *Hokkekyō*), the Buddhist text held in highest regard by Dōgen and medieval Japanese Buddhism in general. Of all the many Mahayana scriptures and Zen epistles to which Dōgen's writings refer, a remarkably extensive list, the *Lotus* easily receives the most attention with at least fifty-three citations. Dōgen designates the *Lotus* the "King of the Sutras," and numerous *Shōbōgenzō* fascicles are direct commentaries on the sutra's doctrines, including "Hokke-ten-hokke" (Lotus turning the lotus), "Shohō-jissō" (True form of all dharmas), "Sangai yuishin" (Triple world is mind only), "Kūge" (Flowers of emptiness), "Keisei-sanshoku" (Sounds of rivers, forms of mountains), and "Yuibutsu yobutsu" (Only between a Buddha and a Buddha). Dōgen's emphasis on the *Lotus* diverges from that of both the Tendai and Nichiren sects, which also revere it, because he views the true meaning of the scripture as being based on the impermanent and nonsubstantial ground of all human affairs and natural phenomena. He expands and reformulates Hui-neng's dictum "The deluded mind is turned by the *Lotus*; the enlightened mind itself turns the Lotus."

This is the one group of waka in the collection for which dating is unclear, although it is likely that the poems were composed in 1241 (the Fukakusa period) at the time of the composition of the *Shōbōgenzō* fascicles we have already cited in this chapter. On the other hand, the poems on the *Lotus* represent the only group that demonstrates an ideological unity and literary progression in commenting on the inner meaning of the scripture and its relation to Zen practice and everyday life. The first waka in the sequence (#3-J) establishes the nonduality of daily time and enlightenment. It expresses two main doctrines: *gyōjū zaga* (the four daily activities of walking, standing, sitting, and sleeping constitute absolute truth), indicated by the phrase *hinemosu ni nasu,* and also expressed by the scarecrow metaphor in #18-J; and *kannō-dōkō* (reciprocal spiritual communion between sutra and disciple, or Buddha and devotee) suggested by the phrase *koe to kokoro,* which is also conveyed by the refined imagery of the linen veil in #28-J. The next poem (#4-J) asserts the universality of the sutra by highlighting the "mystical cry of monkeys" reverberating throughout the mountains, a sound perceived as a kind of chanting of the scripture, perhaps also parodying the traditional poetic idealization of the sound of frogs and deer. This irony sets the stage for the identification in the following poem (#5-J) of the cacophonous marketplace with the serenity of the Dharma and, by extension, of materialism and spiritualism, and the relative and the absolute. The fourth poem in the sequence (#6-J) repeats and reinforces the universality of Buddha. The Buddha is characterized humbly in being referred to as "our Sakyamuni," yet he is also glorified through a deliberately exaggerated personification of the mountain peaks as his body and the valley streams as his tongue. The final waka (#7-J) holds the romantic flavor of the previous poem and undercuts or reduces the meaning to its fundamental transient ground. It is a moral injunction stressing that, although always involved in impermanence, people tend to overlook the opportunity to investigate the inner significance of mundane experience, which invariably discloses its nonsubstantive basis despite people's efforts to resist this truth.

One of Dōgen's Chinese poems, #31-C, also expresses a celebration of the message of the *Lotus*. It is based on the "Hōshi kudoku" chapter of the scripture, which says that reading, reciting, or copying the scripture leads to enlightenment.

Hokkekyō ni daisu   Five poems on the Lotus Sutra
go-shu ni iwaku

3-J

Yomo sugara   Day and night
Hinemosu ni nasu   Night and day,
Nori no michi   The way of Dharma as everyday life;

Mina kono kyō no   In each act our hearts
Koe to kokoro to.[3]   Resonate with the call of the sutra.

4-J

Tani ni hibiki   The mystical cry of monkeys
Mine ni naku saru   Resounding from the mountain peaks,

Taedae ni   Echoing in the valleys below:
Tada kono kyō o   The sound of the
Toku to koso kike.   Sutra being preached.

5-J

Kono kyō no   Attaining the heart
Kokoro o uru wa   Of the sutra,
Yo no naka ni   Are not even the sounds
Urikau koe mo   Of the bustling marketplace
Nori o toku kawa.   The preaching of the Dharma?

6-J

Mine no iro   Colors of the mountains,
Tani no hibiki mo   Streams in the valleys;
Mine nagara   One in all, all in one,

Waga Shakamuni no	The voice and body of
Koe to sugata to.	Our Sakyamuni Buddha.[4]

7-J

Dare totemo	Everyone admires
Hikage no koma wa	A graceful horse
Kirawanu o	Galloping past the streaming sunlight,
Nori no michi uru	But few realize that this fleeting image
Hito zo sukunaki.	Is itself the way of Dharma.

Group 3 "The First Snowfall" (#8-J)

This is the third poem in the collection marking a specific occasion in Dōgen's life—his observation of an early snowfall in the first autumn of his stay at Eiheiji Temple (then known as Daibutsuji). Along with waka #2-J and 34-J on the beauty of the moon, #14-J and 41-J on the rotation of the seasons, and #50-J, 51-J, 61-J, and 23-C on the sorrow of ephemerality, poem #8-J is a clear and forceful expression of Dōgen's affirmation of the role an emotional and literary response to nature plays in the religious quest. The last two lines of the poem also seem to recall the famous opening passage of Ki no Tsurayuki's preface to the *Kokinshū*.

8-J

Kangen ninen kugatsu nijūgonichi hatsuyuki isshaku amari furu ni gyo-ei	On the first snowfall of over one foot on the ninth month/ twenty-fifth day in the second year of Kangen {1244}

Nagazuki no	*Crimson leaves*
Momiji no ue ni	*Whitened by the season's first snow—*
Yuki furinu	*Is there anyone*
Minhito tareka	*Who would not be moved*
Uta o yomazaran.	*To celebrate this in song?*

Group 4 "Doctrinal Poems" (#9-J–20-J)

This group of twelve poems on Mahayana and Zen doctrinal topics and mottoes was bestowed in 1248 at Saimyōji Temple in Kamakura upon the request of Kitano Onkata, Hōjō Tokiyori's wife. Some of the editions preface the sequence by indicating "ten poems," but they still include twelve. Dōgen was apparently summoned by the Hōjō to lecture on his approach to Buddhist theory and practice in the temporary capital of Japan and the center of the Rinzai Zen Five Mountains *(Gozan)* monastic institution. His stay in Kamakura lasted about eight months, from summer 1247 till the spring of the following year. Modern biographers have questioned whether Dōgen actually made the long and arduous crosscountry journey so late in life or had the poems sent in place of making a personal visit. There are no records of other writings for this occasion, and it seems unlikely that the Hōjō himself would have been interested in the noted Zen master as an author of verse. Yet poetry may have been appropriate to the occasion since the "feminine" waka form could have appealed to the Hōjō's wife as well as to the Rinzai priests, who commonly used poetic expression for their teaching. One scholar suggests that only the first poem in the sequence was composed for the Kamakura visit and that the others were grouped with it subsequently.

The general theme of these verses is an uncompromising emphasis on nonduality to eliminate any subtle gap or bifurcation between relative and absolute, impermanence and eternity, and practice and realization. Poems #9-J and 16-J assert the efficacy of language as a manifestation of impermanence expressing the infinite variations of the Dharma. The identity of time and eternity is conveyed in #11-J on the full moment of single-minded concentration; #12-J, which evokes the fleeting quality of things and circumstances; #13-J, suggesting the unity of original and acquired enlightenment; #14-J, highlighting the rotation of distinct yet overlapping seasons; and #20-J, on the perpetual renewal of spring blossoms. Several poems suggest the inseparability of particularity and universality: #10-J, which equates the "true person" and the entire Dharma-realm; #17-J, on the indistinguishability of appearance and reality; and #19-J, through the image of a unswayable boat drifting in the moonlit waters. Finally, #15-J on the traceless flight of the waterfowl and #18-J on the seeming passivity of the scarecrow both express the oneness of everyday activity and enlightenment.

Hōji gan teibi no toshi *Doctrinal poems presented to*
Kamakura ni arite *Kitano Onkata {Hōjō*
Kitano Onkata *Tokiyori's wife} at Saimyōji*
Saimyōji no tonoyori *Temple in Kamakura in the*
dōka wo go-shomō *first year of Hōji {1247}*
no toki *(twelve waka)*

9-J

Kyōge betsuden *Special transmission outside the teaching*[5]

Araiso no *The Dharma, like an oyster*
Nami mo eyosenu *Washed atop a high cliff:*
Takayowa ni *Even waves crashing against*
Kaki mo tsukubeki *The reefy coast, like words,*

Nori naraba koso. May reach but cannot wash it
 away.⁶

10-J

Jinjippōkai True person manifest throughout
shinjitsunintai the ten quarters of the world⁷

Yo no naka ni The true person is
Makoto no hito ya Not anyone in particular;
Nakaruran But, like the deep blue color
Kagiri mo mienu Of the limitless sky,
Ōzora no iro. It is everyone, everywhere in the
 world.

11-J

Kentōkagodō Becoming enlightened upon
 seeing the peach blossoms⁸

Haru kaze ni Petals of the peach blossom
Hokorobi ni keri Unfolding in the spring breeze,
Momo no hana Sweeping aside all doubts
Edaha ni wataru Amid the distractions of
Utagai mo nashi. Leaves and branches.

12-J

Junijijūfukūka Not a moment spent idly in
 twenty-four hours⁹

Sugi ni keru Over forty years so quickly passed!
Yosoji amari wa Day and night following

Ōzora no　　　　　　　　The path of the sun and moon,
Usagi karasu no　　　　　Which, like the hare and scrow,
Michi ni koso ari keru.　Swiftly travel in the heavens.[10]

13-J

Fubo shoshō no manako　**True seeing received at birth**[11]

Tazune iru　　　　　　　Seeking the Way
Miyama no oku no　　　　Amid the deepest mountain paths,
Sato nareba　　　　　　　The retreat I find
Moto sumi nareshi　　　　None other than
Miyako nari keri.[12]　　My primordial home: satori!

14-J

Honrai no memmoku　**Original Face**[13]

Haru wa hana　　　　　　In spring, the cherry blossoms,
Natsu hototogisu　　　　In summer, the cuckoo's song,
Aki wa tsuki　　　　　　In autumn, the moon, shining,
Fuyu yuki kiede　　　　　In winter, the frozen snow:
Suzushi kari keri.　　　How pure and clear are the seasons!

15-J

Ōmushojū nishō　　　**You must awaken the**
go-shin　　　　　　　**non-abiding mind**[14]

Mizudori no　　　　　　　The comings and goings
Yuku mo kaeru mo　　　　Of the waterfowl
Ato taete　　　　　　　　Leave no trace,
Saredomo michi wa　　　Yet the paths it follows
Wasure zari keri.　　　Are never forgotten.

16-J

Furyū monji

Ii suteshi
Sono koto no ha no
Hoka nareba
Fude ni mo ato o
Todome zari keri.

No reliance on words or letters[15]

Not limited
By language,
It is ceaselessly expressed;
So, too, the way of letters
Can display but not exhaust it.

17-J

Sokushin-sokubutsu

Oshidori ka
Kamome tomo mata
Miewakazu
Tatsu nami aino
Ukitsu shiranami.[17]

This very mind itself is Buddha[16]

Is it a mandarin duck
Or a seagull floating?
I can hardly tell:
White crests rising and falling
Between the standing waves.

18-J

Gyōjū zaga

Mamoru tomo
Oboezu nagara
Oyamada no
Itazuranaran
Kagashi nari keri.

Everyday life {walking, standing, sitting, sleeping}[18]

Not seeming to protect
The paddy field,
Scarecrow standing
On the hillside—
By no means useless.

19-J

Shōbōgenzō[19]

Treasury of the true Dharma-eye

Nami mo hiki	In the heart of the night,
Kaze mo tsunaganu	The moonlight framing
Sute obune	A small boat drifting,
Tsuki koso yawa no	Tossed not by the waves
Sakai nari keri.	Nor swayed by the breeze.

20-J

Nehan myōshin[20]	**Wondrous nirvana-mind**
Itsumo tada	Because the flowers blooming
Waga furusato no	In our original home
Hana nareba	Are everlasting,[21]
Iro mo kawaranu	Though springtimes may come and go
Sugishi haru kana.	Their colors do not fade.

Group 5 "Poems from a Grass Hut" (#21-J–53-J)

The title of this group, "Sōan no gūei" (Impromptu hermitage poems), suggests that the waka were composed spontaneously, rather than formally, at moments of aesthetic rapture or introspection in a grass-thatched hut or mountain hermitage setting. There are thirty-three waka in this group. Though some editions indicate "thirty poems," they still include the full group. The word *sōan* (also pronounced *kusa no iho* when used in waka #21-J, 39-J, 42-J, and 46-J) refers to the mountains of Echizen and may specifically indicate Kippōji Temple, where Dōgen spent most of his first year in Echizen before Eiheiji was established and where he also wrote two dozen *Shōbōgenzō* fascicles. The word *sōan* also conveys the category of *yamazato* (mountain retreat) literature, which celebrates the solitude and freedom from worldly contaminations found only in mountain huts and hermitages (see also #31-C–35-C).

The poems are filled with the feelings and experiences of Dōgen's Echizen years, including his inspirations and struggles, recollections and hopes, communion with nature and mixed feelings toward Kyoto, and his priestly duties and private longings. Some of the waka are notable for their expression of religious commitment to the bodhisattva vow: the expression of devotion overcoming any separation between Buddha and worshiper, mind and body, and heaven and earth through the humble gesturing of #21-J, the fusion of refined lyricism and Shinto overtones in #28-J, the affirmation of the role of language in #35-J, and the elegant imagery of #53-J. The bodhisattva ideal is also suggested by the evocation of the functions of priesthood in #32-J, 33-J, and 46-J; the commitment to the vow of compassion in #22-J and 42-J; and the rewriting of Zen doctrinal anecdotes in #45-J, 48-J, and 49-J. Devotionalism is expressed in Dōgen's recollection of key formative experiences in his spiritual quest, such as a chance encounter with the Buddhist teachings in Kyoto in #23-J, the lament for the early deaths of his parents in #31-J, and the occasion of viewing an old Echizen temple in #44-J.

Other poems suggest various aspects of an aesthetic response to impermanence as it is manifested in the mountain seasons. For example, the evocation of poignancy in terms of the cicada's call at autumn twilight in #25-J, the spring fragrance in #27-J, and the early spring sunset in #40-J; the sense of ontological grief at the inevitability of change and loss represented by the morning dewdrops in #50-J, and the withering of natural phenomena in #51-J; the feeling of an overwhelming and irresistible emotional attraction to the beauty of the moon and its shadows in #34-J, and the rotation of the seasons in #41-J; a celebration of the interpenetration of seasons encompassing summer and winter in #37-J, fall and winter in #38-J, and winter and spring in #52-J; the moral exhortation to accentuate each moment despite the passing of things in #24-J, 29-J, and 43-J (recalling the horse image in #7-J); and the disclosure of impermanence as nonsubstantiality in #47-J by transmuting an autumnal epithet, *tsuyu-jimo* (dew-frost), into a symbol of the emptiness of all forms.

In addition, some of the waka demonstrate Dōgen's use of the conventional imagery and syntax of the poetic tradition. A key example is the wordplay that illustrates the efficacy of language consisting in its impermanence in #26-J (recalling #9-J). Verbal associations also evoke the nondifferentiation of illusion and truth in #36-J, appearance and reality in #39-J (recalling #17-J), and delusion and comprehension in #44-J. In addition, Dōgen uses poetic devices, such as the pillow-word *azusa yumi* (lit. "catalpa bow"), which symbolizes spring and amplifies the natural imagery of #40-J; and allusive variation, which gives Buddhist meaning to traditional poetic metaphors in #30-J on the image of the pheasant's tail and in #52-J on the warbler's song.

| *Sōan no gūei* | *Impromptu hermitage poems (thirty-three waka)* |

21-J

Kusa no iho ni	Each moment waking, sleeping,
Nete mo samete mo	In my grass-thatched hut,
Mōsu koto	I offer this prayer:
Namu[22] Shakamuni butsu	Let Sakyamuni Buddha's compassion
Kaerimi tamae	Envelop the world.

22-J

Oroka naru	What can I accomplish?
Ware wa hotoke ni	Although not yet a Buddha,
Narazu tomo	Let my priest's body
Shujō o watasu	Be the raft to carry
Sō no mi naran.	Sentient beings to the yonder shore.

23-J

Ureshiku mo	As on Hollyhock Festival Day,
Shaka no mi-nori no	Chancing to meet Sakyamuni's
Afumi-gusa[23]	Blissful Dharma, however briefly,
Kakete mo hoka no	Would I ever be inclined
Michi o fumabaya.	To follow any other path?

24-J

Yotsu no uma	The four horses of suffering,[24]
Yotsu no kuruma	The four chariots of compassion;[25]
Noranu hito	How can one
Makoto no michi o	Find the true Way
Ikade shiramashi.	Without riding upon them?

25-J

Yama fukami	Rising, as the mountain
Mine ni mo tani ni mo	Peaks and valleys deepen—
Koe tatete	The twilight sound of the cicada
Kyō mo kurenu to	Singing of a day
Higurashi[26] zo naku.	Already gone by.

26-J

Haru kaze ni	Will their gaze fall upon
Waga koto no ha no	The petals of words I utter,
Chirinuru o	Shaken loose and blown free by the spring breeze,
Hana no uta to ya	As if only the notes
Hito no nagamen.	Of a flower's song?[27]

27-J

Azusa yumi	Surely it is spring,
Haru no yamakaze	For the fragrance of flowers
Fuki nuran	Circulated by the mountain breeze
Mine ni mo tani ni mo	Spreads throughout
Hana nioi keri.	The peaks and valleys.[28]

28-J

Tanomi koshi	A traveler in Echizen,
Mukashi no shū ya[29]	Wrapping my sorrow with a linen sleeve;
Yūdasuki	My plea that I be veiled
Aware o kakeyo	By the compassion
Asa no sode ni mo.	Of the original Lord.

29-J

Oroka naru	Following only the deluded path
Kokoro hitotsu no	In the six realms—[30]
Yuku sue o	The futile meandering
Mutsu no michi to ya	Of a mind chasing after
Hito no fumuran.	Its own deceptions.

30-J

Ashihiki no	Long night,
Yamadori no o no	Long as the
Shidario no	Long tail of the pheasant:
Naganagashi yo mo	The light of dawn
Akete keru kana.	Breaking through.[31]

31-J

Mutsu no michi	My companions
Ochikochi mayou	Trekking
Tomogara wa	The six realms—
Waga chichi zo kashi	I recognize my father!
Waga haha zo kashi.	There is my mother!³²

32-J

Shizuno-o no	Even for the humble,
Kakine ni haru no	Spring has burst through the gates,
Tachishi yori	For it is time
Furuse³³ ni ouru	To pluck young herbs
Wakana o zo tsumu.	Flourishing in the passing fields of Furuse village.

33-J

Sanae toru	Transplanting rice seedlings
Haru no hajime no	At the beginning of spring—
Inori ni wa	For that prayer
Hirosetatta no	We celebrate the festival
Matsuri o zosuru.	At Hirose and Tatta shrines.³⁴

34-J

Ōzora ni	Contemplating the clear moon
Kokoro no tsuki o	Reflecting a mind empty as the open sky—
Nagamuru mo	Drawn by its beauty,
Yami ni mayoite	I lose myself
Iro ni medekeri.³⁵	In the shadows it casts.

35-J

Anatōto
Nana[36] no hotoke no
Furugoto wa
Manabu ni mutsu no
Michi ni koetari.

Traveling the six realms,
Seeking the primordial words
Of the seven Buddhas of Nara,
Which are ceaselessly
Pervading all paths.

36-J

Moto sue mo
Mina itsuwari no
Tsukumo gami[37]
Omoi midaruru
Yume o koso toke.

Like tangled hair,
The circular delusion
Of beginning and end,
When straightened out,
A dream no longer.

37-J

Natsu fuyu mo
Omoi ni wakanu
Koshi[38] no yama
Furu shirayuki mo
Naru ikazuchi mo.

Summer, winter,
Both inexpressible:
Across the Echizen mountains
White snowflakes falling,
Thunder crackling.

38-J

Miyako[39] ni wa
Momiji shinuran
Okuyama no

Koyoi mo kesa mo
Arare furi keri.

All last night and
This morning still,
Snow falling in the deepest
    mountains;
Ah, to see the autumn leaves
Scattering in my home.

39-J

Waga iho wa	The white mountain of Echizen
Koshi no shirayama[40]	My winter retreat:
Fuyugomori	A blanket of clouds
Kōri mo yuki mo	Covering the frosted peaks
Kumo kakari keri.	And snowy slopes.

40-J

Azusa yumi[41]	Dispersed, as today's
Haru kure-hatsuru	Spring light fades
Kyō no hi o	Yet stays held taut,
Hikitodometsutsu	Like a catalpa bow:
Ochikochi[42] yaran.	My travels are never ending.

41-J

Hana momiji	Seeing the cherry blossoms in spring,
Fuyu no shirayuki	The crimson leaves of autumn,
Miru koto mo	And the white winter snow—
Omoeba kuyashi	I am at a loss to explain
Iro ni medekeri.[43]	An attraction that never fails.

42-J

Kusa no iho ni	Each moment waking, sleeping,[44]
Okite mo mete mo	In my grass-thatched hut,
Mōsu koto	I offer this prayer—
Ware yori saki ni	Let us strive to save
Hito o watasan.	Others before ourselves.

43-J

Itazura ni	Time—
Sugosu tsukihi wa	In idleness,
Ōkeredo	So easily spent;
Michi o motomuru	For seeking the Way,
Toki zo sukunaki.	It has already vanished.

44-J

Itadaki ni	Magpie building
Kasasagi su o ya	Its nest on his head,
Tsukururan	While a spider's web,
Mayu ni kakareri	Like tiny crabs,
Sasagani no ito.	Covers his eyebrows.[45]

45-J

Koe zu kara	Just at the moment
Mimi no kikoyuru	Ear and sound
Toki sareba	Do not interfere—
Waga tomo naran	There is no voice;
Katarai zo naki.	There is no speaker.[46]

46-J

Kusa no iho	At the beginning of summer
Natsu no hajime no	In my grass-thatched retreat,
Koromo gae	The time for changing robes;
Suzushiki sudare	All that remains to be done
Kakaru bakari zo.	Is to hang out the cool bamboo screen.[47]

47-J

Kokoro tote
Hito ni misubeki
Iro zo naki
Tada tsuyu-jimo⁴⁸ no
Musubu nomi mi de.

Mind has no substance
That one can see;
The only binding
Of the body is
Like the dew and frost.

48-J

Ika naru ka
Hotoke to iu to
Hito towaba
Kaiya ka shita ni
Tsuraraini keri.

If you ask,
What is Buddha?
An icicle
Hanging
From a mosquito net.

49-J

Yo no naka wa
Mado yori izuru
Kisa no o no
Hikanu ni tomaru
Sawaribakari zo.

The world—
Like an elephant's tail
Not passing through the window,
Although no one is there
Holding it back.⁴⁹

50-J

Asahi matsu
Kusaba no tsuyu⁵⁰ no
Hodonaki ni
Isogina tachi so
Nobe no akikaze.

Dewdrops on a blade of grass,
Having so little time
Before the sun rises;
Let not the autumn wind
Blow so quickly on the field.

51-J

Kokoro naki	Even plants and trees,
Kusaki mo kyō wa	Which have no heart,
Shibomu nari	Wither with the passing days;
Me ni mitaru hito	Beholding this,
Ure-e zarameya.	Can anyone help but feel chagrin?[51]

52-J

Hima mo naku	Although white snowflakes
Yuki wa furereri	Are endlessly falling
Tani fukami	In the deepest mountain valleys,
Haru ki ni keri to	The clear song of the warbler
Uguisu zo naku.	Reveals that spring has already come.

53-J

Kono kokoro	Not only earthly blossoms
Amatsusora ni mo	But this mind, pure as the
Hana zo nao	Celestial garden of an immaculate sky,
Miyo no hotoke ni	Offered to all the Buddhas
Tatematsuranan.	Manifest here, there, and everywhere.[52]

Group 6 Supplementary Poems (#54-J–63-J)

The ten poems in this group do not appear in some of the older versions of the waka text, but they are contained in the Tokugawa editions by Menzan and others. They have strong similarities to the other poems in the collection in the use of lyrical imagery, poetic motifs, and literary techniques. Several seem to be too close, in fact, which has lead to speculation that they were actually later emendations created by an ambitious editor. For example, #59-J seems to be a combination of #7-J and 43-J, and #57-J is nearly identical to #55-J, itself a mix of #34-J and 17-J. Yet many of the connections between the supplementary poems and the main collection are interesting and noteworthy. Poem #54-J, whose headnote is identical to that of #12-J, represents a strong affirmation of the role of an emotional response to the mountain beauty of Echizen, similar in rhetorical tone ("do they realize?") to #26-J; in emphasis on aesthetic "attraction" or "stirring" *(medeshi)* to #34-J and 41-J; and in autumnal imagery to #6-J, 13-J, and 39-J, among others. As noted, in #55-J the symbolism of the moon representing the liberated mind recalls #34-J, and the doctrine of the nonduality of appearance, "waves," and reality, "moonlight," it expresses is close to #17-J. Waka #56-J conveys the interpenetration of sound and listener, as in #45-J. Here the headnote makes a direct reference to Zen Master Ching-ch'ing, cited in case 46 of the *Hekiganroku*. The phrase *kokoro naki* (lit. "without heart"), used in its conventional sense to mean the subdued or enlightened state of a priest, appears in a different context in #51-J, where it refers to the trees and plants "which have no heart." The imagery of winter scenery in #58-J based on the relational word *shiro* (white), referring to the white heron *(shirasagi)* lost in the snow, is close in theme and style to the expression of nondifferentiation allowing infinite variation in #17-J and 39-J.

Poems #60-J and 61-J, which deal with the sorrowful and nonsubstantive aspects of transiency, seem to be the most interesting and effective of the supplementary waka. Waka #60-J evokes a deep personal uneasiness and sadness at the inevitable passing of time most poignantly felt as the day fades into night, symbolized by the "firefly's soft glimmer," recalling the cicada's cry of #25-J and the dispersed spring light in #40-J. Poem #61-J, one of the most frequently cited verses in Dōgen's collection, skillfully combines philosophical nuance and lyrical imagery, using the metaphors of moonlight, as in #19-J and 34-J, and of dewdrops suggesting tears, as in #50-J. In this verse the dewdrops, representing infinite particularity and the moon, the source of illumination, are fully and continually integrated by virtue of impermanence.

54-J

Junijijūfukūka	*Not a moment spent idly in twenty-four hours*
Hito shirezu	Do they realize
Medeshi kokoro wa	How my heart is
Yo no naka no	Always stirred
Tada yamakawa no	By the valley streams and lofty peaks
Aki no yūgure.	Under the setting autumn sun?[53]

55-J

Zazen kufū	*Zazen practice*
Shizuka naru	The moon mirrored
Kokoro no uchi ni	By a mind free
Sumu tsuki wa	Of all distractions;
Nami mo kudakete	Even the waves, breaking,
Hikari to zo naru.	Are reflecting its light.[54]

56-J

Kyōsei uteki no koe	*Ching-ch'ing's {Jap. Kyōsei} raindrop sound*[55]
Kiku mama ni	Because the mind is free—

Mata kokoro naki	Listening to the rain
Minishi areba	Dripping from the eaves,
Onore nari keri	The drops become
Noki mo tama mizu.	One with me.

57-J

Zazen

Zazen

Nigori naki	The moon reflected
Kokoro no mizu ni	In a mind clear
Sumu tsuki wa	As still water:
Nami mo kudakete	Even the waves, breaking,
Hikari to zo naru.	Are reflecting its light.

58-J

Raihai

Worship

Fuyu kusa mo	A white heron
Mienu yukino no	Hiding itself
Shirasagi wa	In the snowy field,
Ono ga sugata ni	Where even the winter grass
Mi o kakushi keri.	Cannot be seen.[56]

Sōan no zatsuei

Miscellaneous hermitage poems

59-J

Todomaranu	With time flying by,
Hikage no koma no	Like a horse galloping
Yuku sue ni	Past the streaming sunlight,
Nori no michi uru	There are few who can
Hito zo sukunaki.	Attain the way of the Dharma.[57]

60-J

Yama no ha no
Honomeku yoi no
Tsukikage ni
Hikari mo usuku
Tobu hotaru kana.

A *firefly's*
Soft glimmer,
As the mountain ridge
Faintly appears under the
Dim glow of the moon.

61-J

Mujō

Yo no naka wa
Nani ni tatoen
Mizudori no
Hashi furu tsuyu ni
Yadoru tsukikage.

Impermanence

To what shall
I liken the world?
Moonlight, reflected
In dewdrops,
Shaken from a crane's bill.

Sanko nishu

Two poems from a mountain retreat

62-J

Tachiyorite
Kage mo utsusaji
Tanigawa no
Nagarete yonishi
Iden to omoeba.

In the stream,
Rushing past
To the dusty world,
My fleeting form
Casts no reflection.

63-J

Yama zumi no	The moon
Tomo to hanaraji	Beyond the peak
Mine no tsuki	Is not my companion on this hill,
Kare mo ukiyo o	For it must return
Meguru mi nareba.	To cast its light on the floating world.

Chapter Four

Treading Along in This Dreamlike World:
Selections from the Chinese Poetry Collection

THIS CHAPTER contains translations of representative selections from Dōgen's Chinese poetry collection based on the version that appears in his complete works, the *Dōgen zenji zenshū*. In contrast with the Japanese waka, which uniformly adhere to the five-line waka style, it may be more appropriate to refer to Chinese *collections,* since the Chinese poetry, or kanshi, include several different styles of poetry, although many of these follow the traditional four-line, seven-character pattern. These styles are contained primarily in the *Eihei kōroku* but also appear in other texts, including the *Shōbōgenzō*. The Chinese poetry is the only kind of writing that was composed throughout Dōgen's career, beginning with his trip to China in 1223, and it is also the sole work from this crucial early period in his career. He continued to compose Chinese verse throughout his stay at temples in Kyoto/Fukakusa and in Echizen, and his work culminated in his final death poem.

The vast majority of the kanshi are included in different sections of the *Eihei kōroku*. Unlike the waka collection, which did not appear until the publication of the *Kenzeiki* over two centuries after Dōgen's death, the kanshi were included in the *Eihei kōroku* and were edited by his main disciples, Ejō, Gien, and Senne. But like the *Kenzeiki* and many other texts from the medieval period in Japan, the extant editions or manuscripts stem from a much later time in the sixteenth century (the *Shōbōgenzō* is an exception to this general rule). The main version of *Eihei kōroku* is a text known as the Sozanbon, probably dating from 1598, and there are several other editions and commentaries from the sixteenth and seventeenth centuries, a period of revival for Sōtō scholarship. Again Menzan plays a key role, primarily because he created a popular collection of Dōgen's poetry, known as the *Kuchūgen,* culled from different sections of the *Eihei kōroku.* The kanshi in the *Eihei kōroku* fall into three main divisions: the *jōdō*-style, or poetic comments accompanying sermons; the *sango*-style, or verses on natural and lyrical themes; and the *juko*-style, or verse commentaries on kōan cases. A fourth group of kanshi are miscellaneous poems from the *Shōbōgenzō* and other sources.

The citation in parentheses following each poem number refers to the volume and section number in the *Eihei kōroku* text (for example, EK 1.1).

Group 1 Jōdō-*style Poems (#1-C–14-C)*

These poems appear in the first seven volumes of the *Eihei kōroku,* which contains over five hundred sermons Dōgen delivered over a fifteen-year period that were edited by Dōgen's foremost disciple, Ejō (volumes 2–4), along with Senne (volume 1) and Gien (volumes 5–7). The sermons are short lectures presented to the congregation of monks in the Dharma Hall *(hattō)* of the temple. The first sermons were delivered by Dōgen at Kōshōji Temple in Fukakusa beginning in 1236. Then there was a period lasting over a year during which there were no lectures, because Dōgen left Kōshōji in 1243 and was settling in Echizen. Dōgen resumed the sermons at Eiheiji in 1244, and they became the single most important dimension of his monastic leadership and teaching style during the last ten years of his life.

The format for the sermons, following the Chinese Zen style of instruction, was for the abbot to sit on an elevated seat on the platform of the hall and explicate a kōan, a sutra passage, or an anecdote concerning one of the patriarchs. After the lecture, usually lasting only a matter of minutes and often ending in a question for the monks to ponder, there was a time for general discussion and debate, but these dialogues were not recorded; the text simply mentions that there was a "pause," or that Dōgen spoke again "after a while," often with a poetic comment on the discussion. In general, the poem does not refer directly to the topic previously dealt with but provides an indirect insight into the themes involved. It is clear that Dōgen, as in his composition of waka, frequently turns for inspiration to nature and the turning of the seasons, expressing a kind of joy despite, or, rather, because of, the extent of snow in the Echizen mountains, as in #13-C. Sometimes the entire lecture is simply the poem. In many cases the sermons/poems also include a demonstrative gesture, with the master drawing a circle in the air or throwing down his ceremonial fly-whisk *(hossu)*. According to the early Zen monastic rules, the sermons were to be presented two times a day, in the morning and in the evening. But by Dōgen's era, they were delivered only in the daytime five or six times a month, including holidays and memorial days. Other, more informal or spontaneous sermons were delivered in the evening, even late into the night, in the abbot's quarters *(hōjō)*—this is the sermon style contained in the *Shōbōgenzō*.

1-C and 2-C (EK 1.1)[1]

On the opening of the Kōshōji Temple Dharma Hall, tenth month/fifteenth day, 1236, during which Dōgen reports how he had been enlightened in China under the tutelage of Ju-ching and returned to Japan "empty-handed" (kūshū-genkyō, *that is, without relics, icons, regalia, and so forth, just with his spiritual experience*). Two verses follow:

Every morning, the sun rises in the east;
Every night, the moon sets in the west;
Clouds gathering over the foggy peaks;
Rain passes through the surrounding hills and plains.

2-C (EK 1.1)

Every fourth year must be a leap year;
The rooster crows at dawn.

3-C (EK 1.7)

This poem is the entire lecture:

When a dragon howls in its hidden cave,
The entire universe becomes quiet;
When a tiger roars on a cliff's edge,
A cold valley becomes warm. Katsu![2]

4-C (EK 1.36)

A lecture on the equalization of everyday profane activities, such as breathing and relieving oneself, with the meaning of the sutras and the teachings of the patriarchs. Then "after a while":

Though the bounties of spring are beginning to fade,
The wild fields are vibrant in varying shades of green,
And peach blossoms are in glorious bloom—
Where can I find Ling-yun now that the petals are fluttering like
   clouds floating in heaven?[3]

5-C (EK 1.51)

A brief lecture asking why, since all beings are endowed with Buddha-nature, the Dharma Hall is overgrown with ten feet of weeds. Then "after a while":

Flowers falling even as we turn our admiring gaze,
While weeds keep springing up despite our chagrin.[4]

6-C (EK 1.66)

This poem is the entire lecture:

The gentle hues of spring are
Everywhere apparent in this eastern paradise;
In heaven or on earth,
The season's beauty is nowhere
More fully realized
Than right here.[5]

7-C (EK 3.192)

A brief lecture recalling Yen-tou's saying "A small fish swallows a big one." Dōgen says, "If you want to understand this, listen to my verse":

A small fish swallowing a big one,
Like a Buddhist priest studying the Confucian classics;[6]
It can penetrate the entanglements of buddhas and demons,
And sweep aside the dust collecting on the Law.

8-C (EK 3.223)

A lecture on the saying "Doubting is to the Way what spring wind is to the rain," as symbolized by the dramatic gestures and body language of the patriarchs, such as sticking out one's tongue or raising the eyebrows. Then "after a while":

Outside my window, plum blossoms,
Just on the verge of unfurling, contain the spring;
The clear moon is held in the cuplike petals
Of the beautiful flower I pick and twirl.

9-C (EK 4.279)

A lecture on the ninth month/first day on the importance of zazen as well as the need to cast off meditation if and when it becomes the object of attachment. Then "after a while":

The opening of the petals of plum blossoms
Heralds the beginning of spring after a long winter;
In the sky at dawn
There is only the round, pale moon.

10-C (EK 4.327)

A brief lecture on how the Buddhas transmit enlightenment without attachment, the arhats transmit it without a loss of status, and sentient beings transmit it without going astray. Then "after a while":

In the dead of the night,
The moon low in the sky,
As Sakyamuni enters parinirvana,
The jade forest, turning white,
Cannot play host to
A thousand-year-old crane,
Whose glistening feathers
Fly right by the empty nest.[7]

11-C (EK 5.392)

A lecture on the twelfth month/tenth day recalling second patriarch Hui-k'o cutting off his arm in the snow to prove his dedication to Bodhidharma; Dōgen says he feels deeply moving emotions and profound sorrow causing tears to flow, which dampen his neckband, because there are no longer masters to command respect such as the first patriarch did. His verse:

Snow is falling far and wide,
Each snowflake neither the very same nor completely different from
   the other ones;
Singing and dancing, they chase after each other,
Till the whole universe is made afresh with its new covering,
As the snow even conceals the moon and clouds,
And puts out the flame in our hearth;
All kinds of leaves and flowers respond differently to the cycles of
   the seasons,
Yet remain oblivious to the cold of night or the chill of winter—
So goes the preaching of the Dharma
By the pines in the valleys and the bamboos on the mountains.[8]

12-C (EK 6.432)

An exceptionally long lecture on the importance of zazen practice, in which Dōgen cites the "parable of the arrow" and also quotes Ju-ching, as he often does, who said that "doing zazen is casting off body-mind (shinjin datsuraku), *without the need for burning incense, worship, the* nembutsu *(chanting the name of Amida Buddha), repentance, or sutra recitation." Then "after a while":*

My nose is in line with my navel;
My ears are on the same plane as my shoulders.

13-C (EK 4.473)

A lecture on a saying attributed to Sakyamuni, which suggests that he would leave behind the merit of the white hairs of his eyebrows after his death to benefit his disciples, followed by a verse:

Frosty plum blossoms reflecting the moonlight at the end of winter,[9]
Adding new lustre to the deep snow on this whitened peak;
Here is the vivid image of the enduring Tathagata—
Who can fathom the depths of his virtue
Spreading over countless generations of his followers and their
  descendants.[10]

14-C (EK 7.481)

This poem is the entire lecture delivered on the first month/fifteenth day of 1252:

Snow covering the red blossoms,
Unfettered by the dusty world;
Is it too cluttered even in this secluded mountain—
Who can really say?
When a single plum blossom opens,
Therein is held the awakening
Of the exquisite beauty of spring.

Group 2 Sango-style Poems (#15-C–37-C)

This group is the heart, or the most poetic section, of the kanshi collection. These poems are intended as art, rather than commentary on doctrine, although they often express Buddhist themes, as is the case with the *jōdō* and *juko* styles. They are included in the tenth fascicle of the *Eihei kōroku*, edited by Senne, a disciple who joined Dōgen's community of monks in the Kōshōji period and became after the master's death one of the most important interpreters of the *Shōbōgenzō*. The sango collection itself divides into three groups: five poems known as *shinsan,* which are celebrations of the patriarchs; twenty verses known as *jisan,* which evokes the author's own enlightenment experience, often with a sense of irony or self-deprecating humor as in #16-C and 17-C; and one hundred and twenty poems known as *geju,* which vary as to theme, length, and style but in many cases are further subdivided according to topic and date of composition. The latter group contains numerous verses from Dōgen's stay in China, including some inspired by his mentor Ju-ching or sacred sites; others were composed along with or for other monks or laypersons. A number were written in Fukakusa after Dōgen's return to Japan, but the majority of the geju poems, like the waka, are from the Echizen period, including a series of fifteen verses on the "mountain retreat," suggesting the period of a year's stay in the small hermitage of Kippōji prior to establishing Eiheiji Temple, and a series of twelve verses on daily monastic activities, which is probably from Eiheiji.

The numbering used below to reference the EK sequence in the Japanese text uses *b* to refer to the jisan section and *c* to refer to the geju section (none of the shinsan are included here).

15-C (EK 10.3b)

Accompanying a self-portrait created while viewing the harvest moon on the eighth month/fifteenth day {harvest moon}, 1249:[11]

The mountain filled with leafless trees
Crisp and clear on this autumn night;
The full moon floating gently above the cluster of roofs,
Having nothing to depend on,
And not clinging to any place;
Free, like steam rising from a full bowl of rice,

figure 9. *Self-Portrait*

Dōgen's famous self-portrait done at Eiheiji while viewing the harvest moon, on which is inscribed Chinese verse #15-C.

Effortless, as a fish swimming and splashing back and forth,
Like drifting clouds or flowing water.

16-C (EK 10.10b)

Accompanying a portrait of the master painted at Kōshōji Temple in the late 1230s. This portrait was used as an object of veneration by the assembly.

If you take this portrait of me to be real,
Then what am I, really?
But why hang it there,
If not to anticipate people getting to know me?
Looking at this portrait,
Can you say that what is hanging there
Is really me?
In that case your mind will never be
Fully united with the wall {as in Bodhdharma's wall-gazing meditation cave}.[12]

17-C (EK 10.16b)

My nose higher than a mountain,
My eyes as bright as ocean water,
My head moving freely like a fan,
My feet as pointy as a donkey's;
When I teach in the Abbot's Room,
I like to raise my sweaty fist;
When I preach in the Dharma Hall,
I always need to lean on my staff;
When someone asks for water,
I point to the bucket;
When someone asks for rice,
I offer a bowl;[13]

Previously, I observed the precepts down to the minutest details
Like some kind of trained animal;
Now, even though I wear Sakyamuni's robe,
Everyone in heaven and on earth laughs and calls me an old rice bag.[14]

18-C (EK 10.4c)

A silver mountain crushed and an iron wall ripped apart
In the wake of his menacing glare;
Who is it surveying the damage?
How to describe this creature:
The face of a demon,
The head of a god,
A body covered with red hair;
He looks to be growing horns.[15]

19-C (EK 10. 22c)

Treading along in this dreamlike, illusory realm,
Without looking for the traces I may have left;
A cuckoo's song beckons me to return home;[16]
Hearing this, I tilt my head to see
Who has told me to turn back;
But do not ask me where I am going,
As I travel in this limitless world,
Where every step I take is my home.

20-C (EK 10.23c)

The original mind-ground is at rest,
Naturally at one with the spiritual,
Without ever having to strive for the Dharma;

Experiencing the truth in this body,
Forgetting about labels like "sacred" and "profane,"
The World-Honored One {Sakyamuni} was enlightened
On seeing the bright morning star,
While looking up with a weary but enraptured face.

21-C (EK 10.32c)

On visiting a pious layman mourning the death of his son:

When he opens his true eyes, the pupils are clear;
Looking at his face, he seems steady,
Tears having already been shed,
Though his son has entered the realm of the dead,
Lord Yama!
You won't catch him crying.[17]

22-C (EK 10.45c)

On visiting Mt. Potaloka {considered in popular Buddhism the earthly abode of bodhisattva Kuan-yin (Jap. Kannon)}:[18]

Hearing, thinking, and practice alone
Actualize the mind of original enlightenment;
Whoever sees a vision of a god in a cave—
Ye seekers must come to understand,
Kannon does not abide in this place.

23-C (EK 10.58c)

The unspoiled colors of a late summer night,
The wind howling through the lofty pines—

The feel of the autumn approaching;
The swaying bamboos keep resonating,
And shedding tears of dew at dawn;
Only those who exert themselves fully
Will attain the Way,
But even if you abandon all for the ancient path of meditation,
You can never forget the meaning of sadness.

24-C (EK 10.63c)

A Zen monk asked for a verse:

"Mind itself is buddha"—difficult to practice, but easy to explain;
"No mind, no buddha"—difficult to explain, but easy to practice.[19]

25-C (EK 10.69c)

One of six verses composed in An'yōin Temple in Fukakusa, 1230:

Drifting pitifully in the whirlwind of birth and death,
As if wandering in a dream,[20]
In the midst of illusion I awaken to the true path;
There is one more matter I must not neglect,
But I need not bother now,
As I listen to the sound of the evening rain
Falling on the roof of my temple retreat
In the deep grass of Fukakusa.

26-C (EK 10.70c)

Another verse from Fukakusa:

The cool wind blows by telling of autumn;
The weather is fresh as the harvest arrives,
So full of wonderful fragrances,
Circulating throughout the autumn sky
As I remain in my mountain retreat.

27-C (EK 10.71c)

On a snowy night in spring:

Although I cannot help but be upset
By the peach and plum blossoms covered by snow and frost,
I admire how the pines and bamboos
Watch the dreamlike passage of time without regrets;[21]
You may not be able to tell it from my old hair and skin,
But I am unshaken,
Having given up fame and fortune for so many years.

28-C (EK 10.77c)

On hearing an early spring thunderstorm in Kamakura, third month, 1248:[22]

For six months I've been taking my rice at the home of a layman,
Feeling like the blossoms of an old plum tree covered by the snow and frost,
Exhilarated in hearing the first sound of thunder crackling across the sky—
The five red petals of spring peach blossoms will soon be brightening the capital.

29-C (EK 10.82c)

Ju-ching told the assembly of monks at the time of the

autumn moon (eighth month/fifteenth day through seventeenth day, 1226):

Clouds are scattered in the autumn sky,
But you can see the moon in your mind;
I raise up my hossu and say, "Look!"

He instructed the disciples to write three verses with their fellow monks on the three nights, each verse on one of Ju-ching's lines. This verse was on the night of the sixteenth, based on the line "You can see the moon in your mind":[23]

Contemplating the kōan of the sixteenth-night:
If you wish only to see the physical moon,
Then you will miss the moon-that-is-your-mind;
When you see the brightness of clouds swirling about the moon,
You may think at first that it is the moon itself that you are looking at,
But then you will never behold the actual moon on this autumn night.

30-C (EK 10.90c)

One of six verses on snow:

All my life perplexed by truth and falsity, right and wrong;
Now amusing myself in the moonlight,
Laughing at the wind,
Listening to the songs of birds—
So many years spent idly contemplating
The immense white layer on the mountains;
This winter, all of a sudden,
I see it for the first time as a snow-mountain.[24]

31-C (EK 10.99c)

One of fifteen verses on Dōgen's mountain retreat:

Joyful in this mountain retreat yet still feeling melancholy,
Studying the Lotus Sutra *every day,*[25]
Practicing zazen singlemindedly;
What do love and hate matter
When I'm here alone,
Listening to the sound of the rain late in this autumn evening.

32-C (EK 10.100c)

Another mountain retreat verse:

Transmitting to the east the way the ancestors brought from
    the west,
My daily activities illuminated by the moon and shadowed by
    the clouds;
Because I revere the ancient way of the patriarchs,
The secular dust of worldly customs does not reach
Where I stay secluded in my grass-thatched hut,
On a snowy evening deep in the mountain recesses.

33-C (EK 10.105c)

Another mountain retreat verse:

For so long here without worldly attachments,
I have renounced literature and writing;
I may be a monk in a mountain temple,
Yet still I am moved in seeing gorgeous blossoms
Scattered by the spring breeze,
And hearing the warbler's lovely song—
Let others judge my meager efforts.

34-C (EK 10.107c)

Another mountain retreat verse:

Late in autumn the days are cool and clear;
In the dead of night crickets are chirping
Under the crescent moon,
The cacophony of sound echoing my mixed emotions;
Here I sit, gazing up
At the Big Dipper
Slipping off to the east,
As daylight is about to break.

35-C (EK 10.113c)

Another mountain retreat verse:

In a thatched hut in this deep mountain recess,
Ceaselessly practicing meditation and contemplation,
Yet dust keeps gathering even on this high peak of virtue,
As I long to attain supranormal powers [jinzū] as a follower of
 the Tathagata.[26]

36-C (EK 10.118c)

One of twelve verses on the twenty-four hours of the monastic daily cycle.[27] This verse is from eight A.M., mealtime:

After eating the Monks' Hall and devouring the Buddha Hall,
With a lofty mind and an empty belly,
I enjoy looking out at the cloudy mist;
When you lay out the Buddha's bowl in India
Its finery spreads, like the unfolding sky, all the way to Korea;
I haven't begged from Chao-chou yet,
But I am filled with the rice and tea he offers.[28]

37-C (EK 10.124c)

Another verse on the daily cycle, from eight P.M., a time for zazen:

Doesn't the dog have the nature of a dog?
After all, a shrimp is nothing other than a shrimp;
The man from the T'ang walking barefoot learns to walk in
 the T'ang style,
Paying tribute with an elephant tusk brought all the way from
 Persia.[29]

Group 3 Juko-*style Poems (#38-C–46-C)*

The *juko*-style poems are verse commentaries on ninety kōan cases contained in the ninth volume of the *Eihei kōroku,* edited by Senne. Several kōans are accompanied by two or three verses, and a couple are simply listed without commentary. The *juko* were written in 1236, at the time of the opening of the monks' hall at Kōshōji Temple, when Dōgen's following had expanded dramatically and he was looking for new methods for instructing his disciples in the paradigmatic kōan cases prominent in Zen training in China. During this period he created a collection of three hundred kōan cases known as the *Shōbōgenzō sanbyakusoku,* which is just a listing of kōans without commentary, done in preparation for the development of the *Shōbōgenzō* vernacular prose exegetical method. The *juko* poems follow the model of early Buddhist four-line Sanskrit verses known as *gātha.* The kōan collections in China, such as the *Mumonkan* and *Hekiganroku,* always include a combination of *juko* verse comments and prose comments. This collection marks Dōgen's attempt, early in his career, to experiment with the verse style, but he soon abandoned this method and turned to an exclusively prose style of kōan commentary—with a decidedly eloquent, poetic flavor—in the *Shōbōgenzō* fascicles. Nevertheless, the *juko* collection, completed in the same period as yet another major work, the *Shōbōgenzō zuimonki,* is crucial for understanding Dōgen's thought in the Kōshōji Temple period.

38-C (EK 9.7)

On a kōan dealing with the transmission of enlightenment to the then lay disciple Hui-neng, who, on understanding the meaning of pounding rice, was invited to the master's room to receive his seal of approval:

His eyes are bright and lively even in the dead of the night;
Like the Buddha, an old bhikkhu in India,
When the master transmits his divine powers,
Like an Elephant-king, {Hui-neng} stomps over the trails left
  by a fox.[30]

39-C (EK 9.11)

On a kōan in which master Ta-an says that training to become a Buddha is like seeking an ox and riding it home, and Pai-chang responds that "an oxherder uses his staff to make sure the ox does not wander into someone else's field":[31]

In the morning mist, the farmer's clothes get damp;
When the sun sets in the evening, the faraway mountains look
  ever more remote;
Here I am reciting poems celebrating the snow, moon, and plum
  blossoms,
While drawing pictures of the oxherder returning home at dusk.

40-C (EK 9. 52)

On "the sermon of insentient beings," which can only be heard by insentient beings:[32]

Only insentient beings hear the sermon of insentient beings;
Walls and fences cannot instruct the grasses and trees to actualize spring,
Yet they reveal the spiritual without intention, just by being what they are,
So too with mountains, rivers, sun, moon, and stars.

41-C (EK 9.58)

A rewriting of Ju-ching's verse, cited first here, on the meaning of the sound of the bell:[33]

The bell looks like a mouth, gaping,
Indifferent to the wind blowing in the four directions;
If you ask it about the meaning of wisdom,
It only answers with a jingling, tinkling sound...

Dōgen's version:

The bell is a voice articulating emptiness,
Playing host to the wind blowing in the four directions,
Expressing in its own eloquently crafted language
The tintinnabulation: the ringing of the ringing.

42-C (EK 9.63)

On a kōan in which Nan-chüan, whose powers as a Zen master are supposed to transcend those of local gods, is spotted by the land-deity as he enters a vegetable patch, and therefore he must repent before the deity as well as renew his efforts at meditation:

He once traveled freely, his presence unnoticed by others;
He could not be distinguished from a god or demon;
But finally caught, he confessed that he had lost his spiritual power,

Though in the beginning his comings and goings were far from
any crowd.

43-C (EK 9.71)

On a kōan in which a hermit practicing meditation on his own outside the monastic system responds to the question "What is the meaning of Bodhidharma's coming from the West?" by making a wooden ladle and then drawing and drinking from a mountain stream:[34]

If someone asks the meaning of Bodhidharma coming from
the west—
It is that the handle of a wooden ladle is long, and the valley
torrent plunges deep;
If you want to know the boundless meaning of this,
Wait for the wind blowing in the pines to drown out the sound
of koto strings.

44-C (EK 9.72)

On Ling-yun's verse in which he "removed all doubts" (that is, attained enlightenment) while seeing peach blossoms in bloom, which was questioned by Hsüan-sha (Jap. Gensha):[35]

The bright green color of the peach and plum trees so shiny and
lustrous,
Manifesting in these very branches the same spring of hundreds
of generations;
It is foolish to despise what is close by or to value something that
is far away;
Right now remove all doubts by seeing what you see and hearing
what you hear.

45-C and 46-C (EK 9.77)

On the "fox kōan," in which Pai-chang encounters a mysterious old man in the assembly who has been suffering five hundred incarnations, since the age of Kasyapa (a primordial Buddha prior to Sakyamuni), as a wild fox for having misunderstood and denied the law of moral causality; Pai-chang liberates the ghost-fox/monk with the turning word "there is no escape from causality {even for the enlightened person}." Two verses follow:[36]

For saying that a person of great cultivation does not fall into causality,
What appears in front of a ghost cave is not an ordinary old fox,
But when {Pai-chang} grants him a turning word,
The mountains and rivers are suddenly transformed as a confirmation of his bright future.

46-C (EK 9.77)

What a pity that in the era of Kasyapa
A well-respected buddha was transfigured into a wild fox for five hundred lifetimes,
But when he hears the lion's roar {of Pai-chang},
The constant yelping from his long, drooling tongue ceases once and for all.

Group 4 Miscellaneous Poems (#47-C–48-C)

This group contains two verses that reflect Dōgen's style of writing Chinese poetry. They are taken from sources other than the *Eihei kōroku*. One is Dōgen's death verse, which follows the convention for all Zen masters of explicating at least two main events in poetry, their enlightenment experience and their death. Here

Dōgen rewrites his mentor Ju-ching's poem to stress freedom rather than repentance. Ju-ching's version appears first. The other verse is from *Shōbōgenzō* "Zazenshin" (Prescription for zazen). Here Dōgen rewrites a verse by Hung-chih, a predecessor of Ju-ching who led a movement in China known as "silent-illumination Zen." Dōgen's version stresses the dynamism and spontaneity, rather than the quietude and calm, of the meditation experience.

> *For sixty-six years*
> *Committing terrible sins against heaven,*
> *Now leaping beyond,*
> *While still alive, plunging into the Yellow Springs;*
> *Amazing! I used to believe that*
> *Life and death were unrelated.*

47-C

Death verse, a rewriting of Ju-ching's verse:

> *For fifty-four years*
> *Following the way of heaven;*
> *Now leaping beyond,*
> *Shattering every barrier,*
> *Amazing! To cast off all attachments,*
> *While still alive, plunging into the Yellow Springs.*[37]

48-C

The prescription for meditation

> *Dynamic functioning is the essence of all buddhas;*
> *Functioning dynamism is the essence of all patriarchs,*
> *Spontaneously disclosed without thinking,*
> *Fully manifested without obstruction;*
> *Spontaneously disclosed without thinking—*

*Its spontaneous disclosure is in and of itself fully revealed,
Fully manifested without obstruction—
Its full manifestation is in and of itself completely realized;
The spontaneous disclosure fully revealed in and of itself is
Completely attained without defilement;
The full manifestation completely realized in and of itself is
Completely attained without leaning straight or bent;
Complete attainment is revealed in and of itself without defilement;
Full manifestation is realized in and of itself without loss or lack;
Complete realization is attained in and of itself without leaning straight or bent;
Realization is exerted in and of itself without design;
The water is clear to the very bottom—
Fish swim just like fish;
The vast sky is empty up to the firmament;
Birds fly just like birds.*

APPENDIX A

Selected Bibliography

THE MAIN source for the translation of the poetry collections and other philosophical writings is

Kagamishima Genryū et al., eds. *Dōgen zenji zenshū* (Complete Works of Dōgen zenji). 7 vols. Tokyo: Shunjūsha, 1988–1993.
  Waka collection (*Sanshōdōei*), vol. 7, pp. 52–179.
  Kanshi collection, in *Eihei kōroku*, 10 fascicles, vols. 3 and 4.
  Shōbōgenzō, 92 fascicles, vols. 1 and 2.
  Shōbōgenzō zuimonki, 6 fascicles, vol. 7, pp. 52–151.

Other sources for the waka collection include:

Funetsu, Yoko. "'Sanshōdōei' no meishū, naritachi, seikaku." *Daisai daigaku kokubun* 5 (1974): 24–44.

Hata, Egyoku, et al. "Satori wo utau: Dōgen zenji no uta." *Zen no kaze* 1 (1981): 22–37.

Heine, Steven. *A Blade of Grass: Japanese Poetry and Aesthetics in Dōgen Zen.* New York: Peter Lang, 1989.

———. "Dōgen and the Japanese Religio-Aesthetic Tradition." *Eastern Buddhist* 22/1 (1989): 71–95.

Kawamura, Kōdō, ed. *Eihei kaizan Dōgen zenji gyōjō—Kenzeiki.* Tokyo: Taishūkan shoten, 1975, pp. 82–96. Includes five medieval manuscripts of the *Kenzeiki* in addition to Menzan's *Teiho Kenzeiki.*

Kishizawa, Ian. *Zusuikaian zuihitsu.* Tokyo: Daibōinsatsu, 1960.

Ōba, Nanboku. *Dōgen zenji Sanshōdōei no kenkyū.* Tokyo: Nakayama shobō, 1970.

———. *Dōgen zenji waka-shū shin-shaku.* Tokyo: Nakayama shobō, 1972. A critical edition based on five manuscripts of the *Kenzeiki* in Kawamura, four independent temple manuscripts of the waka collection *Teiho Kenzeiki,* and Tokugawa commentaries, as well as Ōkubo's edition.

Ōkubo, Dōshū. *Dōgen zenji-den no kenkyū.* Tokyo: Chikuma shobō, 1966, pp. 358–63.

———, ed. *Dōgen zenji zenshū* (Complete works of Dōgen zenji). vol. 2. Tokyo: Chikuma shobō, 1970, pp. 411–16. A critical edition based on older manuscripts, *Teiho Kenzeiki,* Tokugawa-era commentaries.

Ōyama, Kōryū. *Kusa no ha: Dōgen zenji waka-shū.* Tokyo: Sōtō-shū shūmucho, 1971.

Sawaki, Kōdō. *Sawaki Kōdō zenshū.* vol. 13. Reprint, Tokyo: Daihōrinkan, 1963.

Shūgen. *Sōtō-shū zensho.* vol. 2, pp. 188–303. Tokyo: Sōtō-shū shūmuchō, 1970–1973. Contains three commentaries on the waka collection: "Monge" (1747), "Sanshōdōei ryakuge" (1853), and "Sanshōdōei-shū kōjutsu" (1882).

Other sources for the kanshi collection include:

Hata, Egyoku. "*Eihei kōroku*—sono sodoku to chūkai," *Sanshō* (1975–1977).

Ōkubo, Dōshū, ed. *Dōgen zenji zenshū*. vol. 2. Tokyo: Chikuma shobō, 1970.

Ōtani, Teppō, ed. *Manzan-bon Eihei kōroku sozanhon taikō*. Tokyo: Issuisha, 1994.

Sawaki, Kōdō. *Sawaki Kōdō zenshū*. vol. 17. Reprint, Tokyo: Daihōrinkan, 1963.

Yokoi, Yūhō, ed. *Gendaigoyaku Eihei kōroku*. Tokyo: Sankibō, 1978.

———, trans. *The Eihei Kōroku*. Tokyo: Sankibō, 1987.

APPENDIX B

Chronology of Dōgen's Life
Based on traditional sources, including the *Kenzeiki*

1200 Born first month/second day in Kyoto of the Minamoto family (parents uncertain).

1202 Father dies.

1203 Reads *Pai-yung*, by Li-ch'iao.

1204 Reads Mao-shih and Tso-chuan.

1207 Mother dies; Dōgen is deeply impressed by the transiency of the world and vows to pursue the Dharma.

1208 Studies the *Kusharon* (Skt. *Abhidharmakosa*).

1212 Declines Mastudono Sonkō's (relation uncertain) offer to train for the ministry; departs for Enryakuji Temple on Mt. Hiei.

1213 Becomes Tendai monk under Kōen.

1214 Experiences a profound doubt about the relation between original enlightenment *(hongaku)* and the need for continuing practice.

1215 Possible meeting at Kenninji with Eisai, founder of Rinzai Zen in Japan.

1223 Leaves for Sung China with Myōzen, Eisai's disciple; receives instruction of "no reliance on words and letters" from the chief cook of Mt. Ayuwang monastery (later recorded in *Tenzokyōkun*, 1237); begins writing Chinese *sango*-style verses.

1227 Receives patriarch seal of Ts'ao-tung (Jap. Sōtō) sect from Ju-ching after earlier experience of "casting off body/mind" *(shinjin datsuraku)*; returns to Kyoto and writes *Fukanzazengi*.

1230 Moves to An'yōin Temple in Fukakusa; writes kanshi verses on retreat.

1231 Writes "Bendōwa," main introduction to his thought.

1233 Opens Kannon Dōri-in Temple in Fukakusa; writes *Shōbōgenzō* "Genjōkōan," first fascicle in many editions.

1236 Opens Kōshōji Temple monks hall in Fukakusa; completes collection of *juko*-style verse commentaries on kōans, and begins *jōdō*-style verses in Dharma Hall sermons.

1238 Ejō completes edition of *Shōbōgenzō zuimonki*, a collection of Dōgen's sermons and anecdotes.

1240 Writes "Uji," "Sansuikyō," and other fascicles.

1241 Writes "Busshō," "Hokke-ten-hokke," others; perhaps time of composing "Hokkekyō go-shu" (Five poems on the Lotus Sutra).

1243 Moves to Echizen Province in July, stays at Kippōji and Yamashibu-dera Temples; most prolific period of *Shōbōgenzō* writing, including "Kūge" (Flowers of emptiness), "Sesshin sesshō" (Disclosing mind, disclosing nature), "Kattō" (Tangled vines); perhaps the beginning of the composition of thirty-three "Impromptu hermitage poems" as well as many *sango* on mountain-retreat themes. This is the key period in Dōgen's career as a poet.

1244 Opens Daibutsuji Temple in July; composes waka on occasion of first snowstorm (ninth month/twenty-fifth day); continues composition of *jōdō* and *sango* verses over next ten years.

1246 Changes name from Daibutsuji to Eiheiji (Temple of Eternal Peace).

1247 By the invitation of Hōjō Tokiyori, visits Five Mountains center in Kamakura, and presents twelve waka on Buddhist topics to the Hōjō's wife at Saimyōji Temple; writes one kanshi at end of trip.

1248 Returns to Eiheiji in March.

1252 Falls ill in autumn.

1253 Departs for Kyoto in the eighth month; composes waka on Kinobe Pass and on the occasion of the harvest moon; composes final Chinese poem at death (eighth month/twenty-eighth day).

APPENDIX C

Dōgen's Influence on Ryōkan

KAWABATA YASUNARI'S Nobel Prize speech cites Ryōkan's waka on the seasons, which is a variation on the "Original Face" verse, as similarly expressive of the "essence of Japan":

Naki ato no	*In remembrance*
Katami tomo kana	*After I am gone—*
Haru wa hana	*In spring, the cherry blossoms,*
Natsu hototogisu	*In summer, the cuckoo's song,*
Aki wa momijiba.	*In autumn, the crimson leaves.*

Note the way that Ryōkan, who deletes the reference to winter snow and the modifier *suzushi*, subtly shifts Dōgen's metaphysical view of impermanence into a very personal statement. The full scope of Dōgen's influence on Ryōkan, which has inspired several recent Japanese studies, encompasses sectarian and philosophical as well as poetic aspects.[1] Many of Ryōkan's Chinese and Japanese poems were inspired by the *Shōbōgenzō*, about which he wrote commentaries during and after his Sōtō monastic training. At least twenty of Ryōkan's waka are based on a dozen of the poems in

Dōgen's collection; that is, twelve of Dōgen's poems can be traced as the direct source of inspiration for one or more of Ryōkan's verses. Ryōkan is often said to be adored by the Japanese for both his inventiveness and his wit (he is known as Daigu, "Great Fool") as well as for his humility, epitomized by his affection for his begging bowl and his compassion for children and the elderly. He is also greatly admired for his diligent study of Chinese and Japanese literary classics, which he emulated in the highest sense by frequently surpassing the originals. Thus the fact that Dōgen had some impact as a poet on one of the most eminent postmedieval authors of verse is an indication of Dōgen's skills as a writer.

An important historical question is how Ryōkan came in contact with Dōgen's Japanese poetry during an era that, although subsequent to the publication of Menzan's text of the *Kenzeiki* containing the waka, is not otherwise known for serious interest in the collection. It seems likely that Ryōkan studied Dōgen's waka during his twelve-year stay at Entsūji Temple (1778–1790), in present-day Okayama prefecture, after he became a monk at the age of eighteen. Entsūji was also the temple where Kakugan wrote one of the main commentaries on Dōgen's waka collection, published in 1853, over sixty years after Ryōkan's departure; Entsūji may have been a center of waka studies in the Edo period. It is clear that Ryōkan was studying the *Eihei kōroku* there as well as hearing lectures on the *Shōbōgenzō*. At that time the *Shōbōgenzō* text was still kept as a house secret among the priestly elite, who disseminated its teachings only through sermons. According to a Ryōkan verse written some years later:

> *When I was in Entsūji long ago,*
> *The Master lectured on the Shōbōgenzō;*
> *Suddenly it deeply aroused my Dharma-seeking mind,*
> *And I tried desperately to carry out its teachings.*

The connection between Dōgen's poems and Ryōkan's waka is so close that many of Ryōkan's waka could be interpreted as being allusive variations *(honkadori),* in which the phrasing and flavor of the original poem is largely retained and a subtle alteration of meaning is highlighted. The poems that influenced Ryōkan include four that can be categorized as devotional, in that they express religious rather than philosophical or aesthetic themes: #21-J and 53-J (two variations were written by Ryōkan) on Buddhist devotion; #32-J (two variations) on agragrian rites for spring; and #42-J (two variations) on the bodhisattva's vow of compassion. Ryōkan's varation of #21-J shows a shift from Dōgen's nondualistic approach toward worship to an apparently other-power stance emphasizing faith in Amida Buddha:

> *Kusa no iho ni*   Each moment waking, sleeping
> *Nete mo samete mo*   In my grass-thatched retreat,
> *Mōsu koto*   I offer this prayer:
> *Namu Amida Butsu*   Hail Amida Buddha,
> *Namu Amida Butsu.*   Hail Amida Buddha!

In addition to this verse, Ryōkan wrote seven other waka that invoke the name and compassion of Amida. This can indicate one of two conclusions about Ryōkan's religious experience. First, Sōtō Zen as practiced in Ryōkan's day may have been based more on an assertion of faith in the Buddha's saving powers than Dōgen originally intended, perhaps due to the missionary work of Keizan and subsequent patriarchs. It is more likely, however, that Ryōkan was also greatly influenced by the third Japanese Zen sect, Obaku, during his stay at Kōshōji Temple when he first joined the monkhood in 1777. Kōshōji, founded by Dōgen in Fukakusa, had been moved to the town of Uji, farther outside Kyoto. Uji is the center of the Obaku sect (as well as the site of one of the most historically and aesthetically prominent Pure Land temples, Byōdō-in of the Fujiwara family). Obaku Zen stresses a method of practice that integrates *zazen* (seated meditation) and *nembutsu* (recitation prayer), interpreting Amida as a seemingly objective reflection of personal realization.

Another interesting verse is Ryōkan's variation of Dōgen's devotional poem (#53-J); it is one of two variations. The original verse provides a nondualistic perspective on human worship and the universal manifestations of Buddha-nature. Ryōkan's waka reads:

Hachi no ki ni	Violets and dandelions
Sumire tanpopo	Mixed together in
Koki mazete	My beggar's bowl,
Miyo no shobutsu ni	Are offered to all the buddhas
Tatematsuriten.	Manifest here, there, and everywhere.

Here Ryōkan emphasizes the poverty and humility of worship by using the images of the begging bowl, with which he had an almost "personal" relationship, as expressed in many of his poems, and of the wildflowers he has picked, which stand in contrast to Dōgen's "celestial garden." Ryōkan celebrates even the "weeds," which Dōgen decries in the opening paragraph of "Genjōkōan." Ryōkan's poem is less exquisite than the original, but his imagery conveys more emphatically the unity of everyday life and enlightenment, perhaps changing the tone from *yōen* (ethereal charm) to *sabi* (withered solitude).

Other themes in poems by Dōgen that influenced Ryōkan include the sense of longing and sleeplessness upon viewing the full moon in #2-J (three variations were written by Ryōkan); the doctrines of traceless enlightenment in #15-J, and of the nondifferentiation and nonsubstantiality of mind and body in #47-J (three variations); the wintery imagery of mountain provinces in #39-J (two variations) and #57-J; and the poignant evocations of transiency in #40-J and 61-J (two variations). Ryōkan's personalization of the seasonal rotation and interpenetration evoked in #14-J (one of two variations on "Original Face") is a fascinating case. In Ryōkan's poem, cited above, objective phenomena appear as a manifestation of interiority, a reflective legacy of his own illumination, thus suggesting a synthesis of self and world and of past, present, and future from the standpoint of one who continues to realize, according to Dōgen's headnote, his true self.

Finally, Ryōkan's profound respect for Dōgen is indicated

in a lengthy Chinese verse on the *Eihei kōroku,* titled "Reading the *Record of Eihei Dōgen.*" In the first three stanzas Ryōkan recalls studying the *Eihei kōroku* while at Entsūji and pondering his relation to the master who had lived five centuries before, as well as why the text, although studied by some priests, was largely ignored and "covered with dust," so that no one any longer inquired whether it was a "jewel or a stone." In the last stanza, Ryōkan expresses his appreciation for the text, or rather his reluctance to show this emotion[2]:

> *One evening sitting by the light, my tears flowing nonstop*
> *Thoroughly soaked through my copy of the* Eihei kōroku;
> *The next morning an old man living next door visited my thatched hut*
> *And asked me how the book got so wet;*
> *As I tried to speak up, my heart was flooded with feelings,*
> *And my mind could not grapple with explaining an attitude that cannot be put in words;*
> *I lowered my head, but then after a while I thought of something to say:*
> *"It was the rain leaking in last night that got my bookcase so soaked."*

NOTES

Chapter One

1. Cited in Thomas P. Kasulis, "The Incomparable Philosopher: Dōgen on How to Read the *Shōbōgenzō*," in *Dōgen Studies,* William R. LaFleur, ed. (Honolulu: University of Hawaii Press, 1985), p. 84. The Kyoto School was started by Nishida Kitarō and also includes Nishitani Keiji; both wrote extensively about Dōgen.

2. Hee-Jin Kim, "'The Reason of Words and Letters': Dōgen and Kōan Language," in *Dōgen Studies,* p. 56.

3. *Dōgen zenji zenshū,* Kagamishima Genryū et al., eds. (Tokyo: Shunjūsha, 1988–1993), vol. 1, p. 240.

4. Ibid., p. 241.

5. Ibid., p. 14.

6. Ibid., p. 320.

7. An analysis of the Japanese rhyme scheme in Dōgen's Chinese poetry in the tenth volume of the *Eihei kōroku* appears in a

series of ten articles in a journal published at Eiheiji by Hata Egyoku, *Eihei kōroku*—sono sodoku to chūkai, *Sanshō* (1975–1977). These journal articles are based on a different version of the text than the one appearing in the *Dōgen zenji zenshū*, which is used in this translation.

8. The relation between Dōgen and Zeami is analyzed in Nishio Minoru, *Dōgen to Zeami* (Tokyo: Iwanami shoten, 1965).

9. Toshihiko and Toyo Izutsu, *The Theory of Beauty in the Classical Aesthetics of Japan* (The Hague: Martinus Nijhoff, 1981), pp. 4–5.

10. See Watsuji Tetsurō, "Shamon Dōgen," *Watsuji Tetsurō zenshū*, vol. 4 (Tokyo: Iwanami shoten, 1977).

11. Kawabata Yasunari, *Japan, the Beautiful, and Myself*, ed. and trans. E. G. Seidensticker (Tokyo: Kodansha, 1969), p. 74 (Japanese original on p. 10).

12. Ibid., p. 13 (my translation). Kawabata cautions against seeing the poem as "no more than an ordinary, commonplace listing of seasonal images."

13. The second Japanese Nobel laureate, Ōe Kenzaburō, has criticized Kawabata and other modern Japanese authors for their nostaligic romanticism in "Japan, the Ambiguous, and Myself" (Aimai-na Nihon no Watakushi), in *Japan in Traditional and Postmodern Perspectives,* ed. Charles Wei-hsun Fu and Steven Heine, (Albany: SUNY Press, 1995), pp. 313–25.

14. Cited by Charles A. Moore, "Editor's Supplement: The Enigmatic Japanese Mind," in *The Japanese Mind: Essentials of Japanese Philosophy and Culture* (Tokyo: Charles E. Tuttle, 1967), p. 296.

15. Kishimoto Hideo, "Some Japanese Cultural Traits and Religions," in *The Japanese Mind,* p. 117.

16. Richard Pilgrim, "The Artistic Way and the Religio-Aesthetic

Tradition in Japan," *Philosophy East and West* 27/3 (1977): 286.

17. *Dōgen zenji zenshū,* vol. 7, p. 17.

18. Ibid., p. 90.

19. As is the case with nearly all Buddhists from the medieval period, the traditional sources do not hesitate to idealize and romanticize key aspects of the life history from birth to death. A revisionist study of Dōgen's biography is in Nakaseko Shōdō, *Dōgen zenji-den kenkyū* (Tokyo: Kokushō kankōkai, 1979).

20. Dōgen was not exposed to the *Mumonkan,* which was composed in 1228, a year after he left China, and which was brought to Japan after his death. Nakamura Hajime notes the cultural difference between the *Mumonkan*'s use of the image of the cool summer breeze, which he says is indicative of an indefinite, remote boundlessness, and the cuckoo in Dōgen's verse, which suggests an acceptance of concrete phenomena that gives an impression of intimacy. Yet Dōgen's image of the clear autumn moon contrasts with the image of crimson leaves in Ryōkan's verse (see Appendix C, page 159) for parallel reasons—that is, Dōgen's affinity with the Chinese mentality when compared with the style of an Edo-period poet. See Nakamura, *Ways of Thinking of Eastern Peoples* (Honolulu: University of Hawaii Press, 1964), pp. 356–57.

21. Kenkō Yoshida, trans., *Essays in Idleness* (*Tsurezuregusa*) by Donald Keene (Tokyo: Charles E. Tuttle, 1981), p. 138.

22. Ivan Morris, *The World of the Shining Prince* (Oxford: Oxford University Press, 1964), p. 123.

23. Katō Shūichi, *A History of Japanese Literature: The First Thousand Years,* trans. David Chibbett (Tokyo: Kodansha, 1979), pp. 233–34.

24. According to the legends, Dōgen's copying of this lengthy text was aided by the tutelary god of Mt. Hakusan.

25. Nishida Masayoshi, *Bukkyō to bungaku* (Tokyo: Ōfusha, 1967), and *Mujōkan no keifu* (Tokyo: Ōfusha, 1970).

26. Konishi Jin'ichi, *A History of Japanese Literature*, ed. Earl Miner (Princeton: Princeton University Press, 1984), vol. 1, p. 7.

27. Masunaga Reihō, trans., *A Primer of Sōtō Zen: A Translation of Dōgen's Shōbōgenzō Zuimonki* (Honolulu: University of Hawaii Press, 1971), p. 3.

28. Kim, "The Reason of Words and Letters," p. 80 n. 8.

29. Cited in Nakamura, *Ways of Thinking of Eastern Peoples*, p. 554.

30. In the *Shinkokinshū* (4:362), *Nihon koten bungaku zenshū*, vol. 26 (Tokyo: Iwanami shoten, 1975–1977).

31. As translated in David Pollack, *Zen Poems of the Five Mountains* (New York: Crossroads, 1985), p. 37. Musō, one of the great Five Mountains poets, is also known for his *Zuimonki*-like admonitions against an intoxication in literary pursuits by "laymen with shaved heads."

32. Cited in Earl Miner, *An Introduction to Japanese Court Poetry* (Stanford: Stanford University Press, 1968), p. 127.

33. On "fukami" see Robert H. Brower and Earl Miner, *Japanese Court Poetry* (Stanford: Stanford University Press, 1961), pp. 231–34; on "michi" see Jin'ichi Konishi, *Michi—chūsei no rinen* (Tokyo: Kodansha, 1975).

34. Cited in Brower and Miner, *Japanese Court Poetry*, p. 269.

35. Ibid., p. 266.

36. In *Nishida Kitarō zenshū*, vol. 4 (Tokyo: Iwanami shoten, 1965–66), p. 6.

37. Karaki Junzō, *Mujō* (Tokyo: Chikuma shobō, 1967).

38. Kenkō, *Tsurezuregusa,* p. 28.

39. In Donald Keene, ed., *Anthology of Japanese Literature,* vol. 1 (Tokyo: Charles E. Tuttle, 1955), p. 207. In the Heian period, Sei Shonogan's *Pillow Book* opens by evoking the four seasons—spring clouds at dawn, summer moon at night, birds crying in the autumn evening, and winter morning frost.

40. *Shōbōgenzō* "Muchū-setsumu" (Disclosing a dream within a dream) and "Hotsumujōshin" (Awakening the supreme mind); see also waka #50-J.

41. Ōba Nanboku, *Dōgen zenji waka-shū shin-shaku* (Tokyo: Nakayama shobō, 1970), p. 338.

42. In *Nihon koten bungaku zenshū,* vol. 7. Dōgen's waka generally displays a tremendous borrowing from the phrasing of earlier poems, which is part of the common technique of "allusive variation" *(honkadori)* that can be interpreted in contemporary terms as the widespread deliberate practice of intertextuality. On the other hand, the extent of this in Dōgen's case has led some scholars to speculate that either Dōgen was not very original, or some of his verses were actually subsequently concocted by his disciples as a way of "honoring" their master; see the discussion in *Dōgen zenji zenshū,* vol. 7, pp. 338–44, based in part on the studies of Funetsu Yoko cited in Appendix A.

43. *Dōgen zenji zenshū,* vol. 1, p. 2. Dōgen's view has some parallels and differences with the secularized view in a famous Chinese verse by Wang Wei:

> *Day after day we cannot help growing older,*
> *Year after year spring can't help seeming younger,*
> *Come let us enjoy our winecup today*
> *Not pity the flowers fallen!*

44. Cited in Honda Giken, *Nihonjin no mujōkan* (Tokyo: Nihon

hōsō shuppan kyōkai, 1978), p. 164. The translation of Teika (*Shūi gusō,* 11:335) is taken from Brower and Miner, *Japanese Court Poetry,* p. 15, which also cites Tomonori's verse (*Kokinshū,* 2:85). Honda cites both Teika and Tomonori in comparison with Dōgen.

45. Cited in Brower and Miner, *Japanese Court Poetry,* p. 359. In other words, *suzushi* means that the experience of a sensation is "cool," in much the same way that the term is used in the contemporary American idiom.

46. Ōba, *Dōgen zenji waka-shū shin-shaku,* p. 110.

Chapter Two

1. In Keene, *Anthology of Japanese Literature,* vol. 1, p. 206.

2. Kenkō, *Tsurezuregusa,* p. 7.

3. *Dōgen zenji zenshū,* vol. 5, p. 40.

4. Ibid., vol. 2, p. 464.

5. Brower and Miner, *Japanese Court Poetry,* p. 216.

6. Morris, *The Tale of the Shining Prince,* p. 124.

7. Fujiwara Teika, "Maigetsushō," in *Nihon kagaku taikei,* N. Sasaki, ed., vol. 3 (Tokyo: Iwanami, 1935), p. 347.

8. Cited in Brower and Miner, *Japanese Court Poetry,* p. 216.

9 Kenkō, *Tsurezuregusa,* p. 77.

10. Brower and Miner, *Japanese Court Poetry,* pp. 310 and 475.

11. *Dōgen zenji zenshū,* vol. 1, p. 3.

12. Teika, "Maigetsushō," p. 349.

13. In Brower, trans., *Fujiwara Teika's Hundred-Poem Sequence of the Shōji Era,* 1200 (Tokyo: Sophia University Press, 1978), p. 70. *Kokoro* changed from "heart" to "mind" for consistency.

14. *Dōgen zenji zenshū,* vol. 2, p. 539.

15. Ibid., vol. 1, p. 262.

16. Konishi, "Michi and Medieval Writing," in *Principles of Classical Japanese Literature,* ed. Earl Miner (Princeton: Princeton University Press, 1985), p. 204. This approach is also evoked in "Aix en Provence"—"Spring" by the modern poet Kenneth Rexroth, who writes:

> {The tree} isn't an image of
> Something. It isn't a symbol of
> Something else. It is just an
> Almond tree, in the night."

In *The Collected Shorter Poems of Kenneth Rexroth* (New York: New Directions, n.d.), pp. 323–24 (thanks to David Barnhill for calling this to my attention).

17. Cited in Izutsu and Izutsu, *The Theory of Beauty in the Classical Aesthetics of Japan,* p. 22.

18. *Shinkokinshū* (1:35), in *Nihon koten bunagaku zenshū,* vol. 26.

19. Brower and Miner, *Japanese Court Poetry,* p. 476.

20. My translation of: "Utsutsu o mo/ Utsutsu to sara ni/ Oboeneba/ Yume o mo yume to/ Nanika omowan." The original from Saigyō's *Sankashū,* no. 1606, appears in William R. LaFleur, *The Karma of Words* (Berkeley: University of California Press, 1983), p. 6.

21. In Brower and Miner, *Japanese Court Poetry,* p. 269.

22. Morris, *The Tale of the Shining Prince,* p. 126.

23. *Dōgen zenji zenshū,* vol. 6, p. 14.

24. Ibid., vol. 2, p. 536.

25. Ibid., vol. 1, p. 450.

26. Teika, "Maigetsushō," p. 359.

27. *Dōgen zenji zenshū,* vol. 2, p. 197.
28. Ibid., vol. 1, p. 273.
29. Ibid., vol. 2, p. 77.
30. Ibid., vol. 1, p. 301.
31. Kim, *Dōgen Kigen—Mystical Realist* (Tucson: University of Arizona Press, 1975), p. 59.
32. Cited in LaFleur, "Saigyō and the Buddhist Value of Nature," second of two parts, *History of Religions* 13/2 (1973): 239, based on Ienaga Saburō, *Nihon shisō ni okeru shūkyōteki shizenkan no hatten* (Tokyo: Kōdansha, 1944).
33. *Dōgen zenji zenshū,* vol. 2, p. 70.
34. As discussed in Robert Bellah, "Ienaga Saburō and the Search for Meaning in Modern Japan," in *Changing Japanese Attitudes Toward Modernization,* ed. Marius Jansen (Princeton: Princeton University Press, 1965), p. 392.

Chapter Three

1. (#1-J) Kinobe Pass, also pronounced *Kinome,* is a steep precipice on the way between Kyoto and Echizen that Dōgen must have crossed two times—on his move from and his return to the capital.
2. (#2-J) The poem can be interpreted as referring to an anticipation of next year's harvest moon, which, considering Dōgen's illness, probably would never be seen, rather than Kyoto's moon, which symbolizes his return to the capital.
3. (#3-J) The alliteration of *koe to kokoro to* (lit. "sound and heart") following *kono kyō* (this sutra) can be interpreted as suggesting Dōgen's doctrine of "reciprocal spiritual communion between master and disciple" *(kannō-dōkō).*

4. (#6-J) In the holograph of the *Shōbōgenzō,* Dōgen's calligraphy of this poem accompanies the fascicle "Keisei-sanshoku" (Sounds of the valleys, colors of the mountains), which includes commentary on a Zen enlightenment poem attributed to a layman disciple of master Chang-tsung:

> *The sounds of the valley stream his long tongue,*
> *The changing colors of the mountains his blissful body;*
> *Since last night I have heard 84,000 hymns,*
> *But how can I explain them all to people the following day?*

5. (#9-J) The title here and in #16-J alludes to the famous formulation of Zen enlightenment attributed to Bodhidharma:

> *A special transmission outside the teaching,*
> *No reliance on words and letters,*
> *Direct pointing to the heart/mind,*
> *Seeing-into {one's own} nature and attaining Buddhahood.*

The word *teaching (kyō)* can also refer specifically to "sutra" or "scripture." The traditional meaning of the headnote phrase, according to the interpretations of Zen masters such as Te-shan and Ta-hui, tends to negate the role of language in Zen training and transmission. Dōgen's view reverses that approach by stressing the efficacy of discourse and symbol in expressing the Dharma.

6. (#9-J) The phrase *kaki mo tsukubeki* is a complex wordplay suggesting that "the oyster has been cast out of the water" as well as the twofold implication that "language or writing must reach/exhaust the Dharma." Thus the Dharma expresses yet transcends discourse. Also *nori* means "seaweed" in addition to "Dharma," thereby creating an association with the seacoast imagery throughout the poem.

7. (#10-J) An allusion to the Zen saying of master Ch'en-sha,

also mentioned in the *Shōbōgenzō* "Shohō-jissō" (True form of all dharmas) fascicle.

8. (#11-J) An allusion to the anecdote, cited in "Keisei-sanshoku," concerning Zen Master Ling-yun (Jap. Reiun), who, during an arduous mountain journey, gained enlightenment through observing the spring peach blossoms in bloom. In *Shōbōgenzō* "Udonge" (Udambara flower), Dōgen notes Ju-ching's comment, "Ling-yun gained enlightenment upon seeing the blossoms in bloom, but I gained enlightenment upon seeing them fall." Ling-yun's saying also suggests Sakyamuni's experience on the dawn of his awakening when he gazed at the morning star with singleminded concentration free from hindrance or distraction. See also #4-C and 44-C.

9. (#12-J) A moral injunction frequently used in *Shōbōgenzō zuimonki*.

10. (#12-J) The phrase "forty years" alludes to Dōgen's age at the time of composition, and the animals are an image commonly used in Chinese poetry to represent impermanence.

11. (#13-J) An allusion to a passage from chapter 19 of the *Lotus Sutra*; the poem also recalls the parable of the prodigal son from chapter 4 of the *Lotus*.

12. (#13-J) *Miyako* is a pivot-word meaning "home" or "capital," making an association with *sato* ("village," also suggesting *satori*). *Mi ya ko* also means "body and child," which associates with *miyama* (deep mountains), and conveys the unity of original and acquired enlightenment.

13. (#14-J) A Zen motto attributed to sixth patriarch Hui-neng, alluding to the doctrine of *shohō-jissō* (true form of all dharmas) expressed in the *Lotus Sutra*. The poem may also allude to case 19 of the *Mumonkan*, in which the poetic comment on the expression "Ordinary mind is Tao," evokes comparable seasonal imagery. But there are other precedents

for the waka in Chinese poetry and in Kūkai's works, as well as similar verses by Daitō and Ryōkan written after Dōgen's poem.

14. (#15-J) An allusion to the line of the *Diamond Sutra* that is said to have led to Hui-neng's satori upon his having heard it recited. The image of the traceless flight of the bird, evoked by a wide variety authors, including the Taoist philosopher Chuang Tzu, Chinese Zen Masters Tung-shan and Hung-chih, and the Japanese Pure Land author Chōmei, among others, also appears in "Genjōkōan."

15. (#16-J) See note 5 above. A strictly literal rendering of this poem has a quite different meaning, suggesting the traditional Zen view that words and letters are inherently limited: "Because [the Dharma] is outside of language, words and letters also leave no trace on it." Such a translation, however, tends to overlook the context and implications of Dōgen's understanding of the efficacious role language plays in expressing the Dharma, as suggested by waka #3-J, 8-J, 9-J, 26-J, and 35-J, as well as the "Bendōwa" passage: "Let [enlightenment] go and it fills your hands—it is unbound by singularity or multiplicity. Speak and it has already filled your mouth—it is not restricted by lesser or greater."

16. (#17-J) An allusion to Zen Master Ma-tsu's well-known reply to the question "What is Buddha?" "Mind," however, is neither a mental phenomenon nor an individual possession. Rather, mind signifies the universal manifestations of Buddha-nature. At a later time Ma-tsu said, "No mind, no Buddha." See kanshi #24-C.

17. (# 17-J) *Shiranami* (lit. "white waves") makes an association with *kamome* (seagull).

18. (#18-J) The traditional Buddhist doctrine, also expressed in #3-J, that each and every aspect of daily activity is the

continual unfolding of enlightenment experience. The apparent passivity of the scarecrow, symbolic of zazen, at once conceals and reveals the perpetual exertion accomplishing its task.

19. (#19-J) The phrase *shōbōgenzō nehan myōshin* (wondrous nirvana-mind of the treasury of the true Dharma-eye) in the headnote for this and the following waka is also the source of the titles of Dōgen's major philosophical work and his kōan collection. It asserts the capacity for realization of the True Dharma in a historical period considered by many of Dōgen's Kamakura-era Buddhist contemporaries to be an Age of Decline, during which people were separated from the original teachings of the Buddha and incapable of complete enlightenment. *Shōbōgenzō* (Chin. *Cheng-fa yen-tsang*) is also the title of the 1147 collection of kōans by Ta-hui, whom Dōgen frequently criticizes for a misuse of kōan practice. In #19-J the independence and strength of the solitary vessel perhaps suggests Dōgen's status during his mission to Kamakura.

20. (#20-J) See note 19.

21. (#20-J) Unaffected by birth and death; it does not mean eternity in the sense of being the opposite of impermanence.

22. (#21-J) Although the word *namu* (hail) here is reminiscent of the invocation used in *nembutsu* worship of the Pure Land school, Dōgen does not express an other-power *(tariki)*, in contrast to self-power *(jiriki)*, standpoint but evokes devotion as a collective manifestation of all beings beyond the dichotomies of Buddha and devotee, self- and other-power.

23. (#23-J) *Afumi* is a pivot-word meaning both "I encounter" and "hollyhock festival" *(aoi matsuri)* in Kyoto; *gusa* (lit. "grass") indicates both the seasonal background and the motif of travel.

24. (#24-J) An allusion to the "four sights" of Sakyamuni—old

age, illness, death, and meditation—that initially awakened his sense of suffering and pursuit of enlightenment. It also alludes to the anecdote in *Shōbōgenzō* "Shime" (Four horses) categorizing human sensitivity in terms of four cases: those stimulated by the death of any other anonymous person, by the death of a neighbor, by the death of a relative, or by confrontation with one's own dying.

25. (#24-J) A reference to the "advanced teaching" of the Tendai and Kegon doctrines, which synthesize the "three vehicles" *(triyana)* into "one vehicle" *(ekayana)*.

26. (#25-J) The pivot-word *higurashi* means both "cicada" and "the setting of the day," also indicated by the phrase *kyō mo kurenu*.

27. (#26-J) The personification "flower's song" *(hana no uta)* makes an association with "petals of words" *(koto no ha)*, highlighting the twofold nature of language. From a conventional standpoint Dōgen criticizes philosophical discourse and poetic symbolism as being no more than mere ornaments or artifice like shimmery blossoms in the spring breeze. Yet the deeper significance of the association between words and flowers indicates that language, as a manifestation of impermanence, is fully identical with the true realization of the Dharma.

28. (#27-J) The poem can be interpreted along the lines of the parable of Zen Master Pao-che's (Jap. Hōtetsu) fan used in "Genjōkōan," indicating that the pervasive fragrance of blossoms symbolizes the universal manifestations of Buddha-nature, which must ever be circulated by the spring breeze.

29. (#28-J) The Shinto overtones of the phrase *mukashi no shū* (lit. "lord of old") seem to suggest the Buddhist doctrine of assimilation, or *shinbutsu shūgō* (unity of Shinto gods and Buddhist deities).

30. (#29-J) Refers to the various levels of sentient beings, including gods, titans, hungry ghosts, denizens of hell, and animals, in addition to humans, who are all subject to the bondage of *samsara;* also used in #31-J.

31. (#30-J) An allusive variation of a famous waka included in *Hyakunin isshu* about departed or unrequited love. Here, the imagery suggests the doctrine of *honshō myōshū* (identity of original enlightenment), symbolized by the dawn's light, and sustained exertion, suggested by the night of meditation.

32. (#31-J) This seems to represent a personal lament for the early death of Dōgen's parents, which he frequently remarks instilled in him a profound sense of the pervasiveness of impermanence.

33. (#32-J) *Furuse* is a place name but also means "old fields," suggesting the rootedness of rural tradition, as well as "passing world," indicating the continuity of time underlying change.

34. (#33-J) Located in Nara prefecture.

35. (#34-J) The final line, identical to the conclusion of #41-J, indicates a wordplay on *iro* (form; Skt. *rupa*) and *ōzora* (open sky, suggesting emptiness; Skt. *sunyata*), apparent opposites primordially inseparable as manifestations of Buddha-nature.

36. (#35-J) *Nana* means "seven," but the word appears in some editions as *Nara,* the original capital and Buddhist center of Japan, suggesting the primordial source of the wisdom and discourse of the seven primordial buddhas culminating in Sakyamuni as celebrated in the lore contained in the vast literature of Zen "transmission of the lamp" hagiographies, thereby making an association with *furugoto* (lit. "old words"). The poem recalls the notion in Dōgen's *Tenzokyōkun* that the meaning of "words and letters" *(monji)* is "nothing concealed throughout the entire universe."

37. (#36-J) *Tsukumo gami* is a pivot-word that signifies "ninety-nine hairs," and by extension "multitude" and "aging," thus conveying a sense of entanglement amplified by an association with the twofold meaning of *toke* as "to explain (the dream)" and "to unravel (the tangled hair)."

38. (#37-J) *Koshi* means "to cross," and it is also the first character in the name Echizen (also used in #28-J and 39-J).

39. (#38-J) As in #13-J, *miyako* implies both home and the capital.

40. (#39-J) *Shirayama* literally means "white mountain," but it can also be pronounced *Hakusan,* the name of a famous snow-covered peak in Echizen that influenced Dōgen's religiosity and inspired many Court poems on the theme of travel.

41. (#40-J) The pillow-word for spring, literally "catalpa bow," is modified by the verb *hikitodometsutsu* (to hold or draw back).

42. (#40-J) *Ochikochi* is a pivot-word that literally means "hither and thither," and it also suggests "regret" *(oshimu),* perhaps for the loss of time and for the absence from Kyoto.

43. (#41-J) See note 35.

44. (#42-J) This poem seems to be a combination of #21-J and 22-J.

45. (#44-J) The concluding phrase, literally "spider's web," is a pillow-word for "crabs," an image that amplifies the sense of deterioration. Although not actually identified by the diction, the poem seems to refer to a Buddha statue that has been covered and defiled by birds and insects, probably referring to an actual incident when Dōgen visited an old mountain temple during his first summer in Echizen and was struck by the imperturbable presence of a Buddha statue despite obvious signs of decay and disrepair in the temple.

46. (#45-J) A literal rendering: "Because when the sound enters the ear naturally on its own, there is no conversation between friends." In some editions, the fourth line is a negation indicating "there is no conversation and no friends." This poem apparently alludes—though less directly than #56-J—to case 46 of the *Hekiganroku,* in which Zen Master Ching-ch'ing (Jap. Kyōsei) claims not to "hear" the sound of raindrops because he is one with them.

47. (#46-J) This refers to the ritualistic changing of garments and windows on the fourth month, first day for summer and tenth month, first day for winter. The screen seems to symbolize separation, allowing for an interpenetration of interior and exterior, and subject and object.

48. (#47-J) *Tsuyu-jimo* (lit. "dew-frost") is a common epithet for autumn, which here seems to represent the nonsubstantiality of the body, which is primordially indistinguishable from the invisibility of the mind.

49. (#49-J) Alludes to case 38 of the *Mumonkan,* in which the tail of the oversized animal implausibly pushed through a window symbolizes the subtle entanglements of discursive attachment, the final obstacle to the attainment of enlightenment.

50. (#50-J) *Tsuyu* (dewdrops) also suggests the falling tears of sorrow.

51. (#51-J) The rhetorical tone of the final line recalls the conclusion of poem #8-J on the universality of a poetic response to nature and the role of emotions in the religious quest.

52. (#53-J) The final line renders the word *miyo,* a Buddhist term that means both the "triple world" of desire, form, and formless and the "three stages" of past, present, and future.

53. (#54-J) Recalls #8-J, 34-J, 41-J, and 51-J.

54. (#55-J) The image of the waves in this verse appears to be inconsistent with the moon metaphor; the image may be used more effectively in #57-J.

55. (#56-J) An allusion to case 46 of the *Hekiganroku;* see note 46.

56. (#58-J) The imagery recalls #39-J.

57. (#59-J) Seems to be a variation on #7-J.

Chapter Four

1. (#1-C) In some versions of the text this is the opening passage of the *Eihei kōroku,* and in other versions it appears in *Eihei kōroku* 1.48.

2. (#3-C) *Katsu* refers to an exclamatory sound that Zen masters were known to make to stir or even shock their disciples into an experience of awakening—in other words, the dragon's howl and the tiger's roar.

3. (#4-C) A pun on Ling-yun's name, which literally means "spirit clouds"; see also #44-C.

4. (#5-C) This short verse is quite similar to the fourth and final sentence in the opening paragraph of "Genjōkōan"; see Chapter One for a discussion of this passage. The first line is from a Zen saying in chapter 25 of the *Keitoku Dentōroku* text.

5. (#6-C) This verse is a celebration of the independence of Kōshōji Temple and its community of followers.

6. (#7-C) Here and in the *Shōbōgenzō,* Dōgen refutes the notion, which was prevalent in Chinese Zen, of the "unity of three teachings" of Buddhism, Confucianism, and Taoism.

7. (#10-C) This verse is based on a legend, especially popular in

Japan, that at the time of Sakyamuni's death a jade forest turned white as all living beings mourned the loss while a crane symbolizing immortality continued to fly by overhead.

8. (#11-C) The impassivity of pines and the bamboos here and in #23-C and 27-C are common images of timelessness in Chinese poetry, because of the way they nobly and imperviously endure the harshest climatic conditions.

9. (#13-C) The fragrant plum blossoms, referred to quite often in this collection, are a common image, especially in China but also in Japan, for the turning of the seasons—their blooming at the tail end of winter signals that the spring has already arrived.

10. (#13-C) This refers to the image of the Zen institution as a family system, with father(s) and children; it is largely borrowed from the Confucian worldview.

11. (#15-C) This verse accompanying the self-portrait at Hōkyōji Temple in Echizen is based on a similar verse by Hung-chih, an important predecessor of Ju-ching, in the *Taishō shinshū daizōkyō* 48.106.b, as discussed in Ōkubo Dōshū, *Dōgen zenji-den no kenkyū* (Tokyo: Chikuma shobō, 1966), p. 384.

12. (#16-C) The first patriarch is said to have meditated while facing the wall of a cave for nine years until his limbs, no longer needed, fell off. This scene is a symbol of the determination required for sustained zazen practice.

13. (#17-C) The poem refers to *Hekiganroku* case 50 in which a monk asks Yün-men, "What is every atom *samadhi*?" and Yün-men responds, "Rice in the bowl, water in the bucket."

14. (#17-C) Note the self-deprecating humor, typical of Zen masters who are also known to boast with tongue-in-cheek bravado, as in the opening lines of #36-C.

15. (#18-C) This verse seems to evoke Bodhidharma, known for his disdain for ignorance. He was referred to in a duplicitous insult as a "barbarian" because he came to China from the "West," perhaps India or Persia (where Buddhism had spread along the Silk Road in early medieval times). See also #37-C.

16. (#19-C) The cuckoo's sound is a common image in Chinese verse, suggesting a positive, much-welcomed reminder of the need to return home, but its meaning is reversed by Dōgen, the Zen wanderer.

17. (#21-C) Lord Yama refers to the keeper of the land of death in Indian and Buddhist mythology. This is a highly ambiguous verse. According to the translation presented here, the bereaved father has transcended emotion because he sees into the unity of life and death. But the imagery is vague, and if the tears are interpreted as falling now, rather than as having already been shed, the verse could be rendered so as to suggest an almost opposite meaning:

> *Images of his son appearing like phantasmagoria,*
> *In the tears of sorrow welling up*
> *In the pupils of his eyes,*
> *Just now the boy appears to enter into the realm of the dead;*
> *Let not Lord Yama be aware of his entrance!*

18. (#22-C) This poem refers to Dōgen's visit to one of several mountains in a sacred network in China considered to be the abodes of bodhisattvas. The Kuan-yin mountain is on an island just east of mainland China not far from the temple where Dōgen trained under Ju-ching.

19. (#24-C) This verse alludes to the sayings of Ma-tsu, who was famous for the teaching "Mind itself is buddha," recorded in *Mumonkan* case 30, which he later reversed by saying, "No mind, no buddha," in a dialogue with one of his main

disciples, Ta-mei, in *Mumonkan* case 33. According to a commentary on Dōgen's poem, both sayings are difficult to understand and practice if one is unenlightened, but if one is enlightened, there is no need to rely on either phrase.

20. (#25-C) The phrase "in a dream" *(muchū)* evokes the *Shōbōgenzō* fascicle "Muchū-setsumu" (Disclosing a dream within a dream).

21. (#27-C) See note 8 above.

22. (#28-C) Dōgen's trip to Kamakura lasted from the eighth month/ninth day, 1247, to the third month/third day, 1248; in addition to twelve waka (#9-J–20-J), this is the only writing from the period, although a sermon in *Eihei kōroku* 3.251 records Dōgen's feelings on his return to Eiheiji.

23. (#29-C) This poem is particularly interesting for two reasons. First, it shows Ju-ching creating a poetry contest among his disciples—in an earlier time Hui-neng gained the patriarchy by winning such a competition. Also Dōgen's verse is probably the first demonstation of his ability to rewrite creatively the words of the patriarchs with an implicit criticism of Ju-ching's idealist vision by stressing the "actual autumn moon" in the last line.

24. (#30-C) An alternative rendering of the last two lines:

> *I realize that the snow piled high*
> *Is itself nothing other than the mountain.*

25. (#31-C) This refers to the nineteenth chapter of the *Lotus Sutra* entitled "Hōshi kudoku" (The Merits of the Dharma-preacher), which asserts that any use of the sutra, including reading, citing, or copying, has merits that help enlighten all living beings.

26. (#35-C) The last line may be interpreted to mean "my plea is

to be saved by the supranormal powers of the Tathagata."

27. (#36-C–37-C) This sequence of poems covers every activity from sleeping and dreaming to eating, chores, and meditation.

28. (#36-C) A reference to a kōan cited in *Shōbōgenzō* "Kajō" (Daily activity) and in Dōgen's *Shōbōgenzō sanbyakusoku* collection (no. 233) in which Chao-chou (Jap. Jōshū) gives the same response, "Drink tea," whether monks answer yes, no, or maybe to one his queries.

29. (#37-C) The first line evokes the famous "Mu" kōan in which Jōshū answers *Mu* (No!) to the question of whether a dog has Buddha-nature. The last two lines refer to Bodhidharma, who came to China in the T'ang dynasty from Persia bearing the valuable gift of a tusk, symbolizing Zen wisdom; see also note 15.

30. (#38-C) The fox, a folklore symbol of deception and betrayal, represents a misguided or arrogant form of Zen practice that needs to be repudiated by authentic masters; see #45-C and 46-C on the "fox kōan."

31. (#39-C) The image of oxherding as a symbol of the process of attaining enlightenment is made famous in the series of Ten Oxherding Pictures, in which the oxherder returns to the marketplace (that is, *samsara*) after having first tamed the beast and reverted to a realm of primordial nothingness.

32. (#40-C) Dōgen devotes a chapter to this topic, one of the main tenets of the Mahayana Buddhist doctrine of universal Buddha-nature, in the *Shōbōgenzō* "Mujō-seppō" (Sermon of insentient beings) fascicle.

33. (#41-C) The theme of the ringing of the bell is an important image discussed extensively in *Shōbōgenzō* "Inmo" (Suchness) and also cited in "Makahannyaharamitsu" (Great perfection of wisdom).

34. (#43-C) A common theme in Zen kōans, as in *Mumonkan* case 11, is the testing of irregular practitioners by Zen masters who generally seek to prove their own superiority while acknowledging the insights attained by all those who do *zazen,* even outside the confines of the monastic compound.

35. (#44-C) Dōgen returns to the topic of Ling-yun's enlightenment, as in #11-J and 4-C.

36. (#45-C) The "fox kōan" draws on the folklore imagery of spirit possessions by magical foxes, which require an exorcism performed by a Buddhist priest, and it is also one of the few cases that deals specifically with a traditional Buddhist philosophical concept: the meaning of causality and its relation to enlightenment (noncausality). See my article, "Putting the 'Fox' Back in the 'Wild Fox Kōan': The Intersection of Philosophical and Popular Religious Elements in the Ch'an/Zen Kōan Tradition," *Harvard Journal of Asiatic Studies* 56/2 (1996): 257–317.

37. (#47-C) Yellow Springs is a conventional term for the netherworld or for entrance to the land of the dead, or hell.

Appendix C

1. For a comparative listing of Dōgen's waka specifically used as the basis of variations by Ryōkan, see Sakei Tokumoto's afterword, "Kaisetsu," in *Sawaki Kōdō zenshū* (Tokyo: Daihōrinkan, 1963), vol. 13, pp. 347–50. (Vol. 13 contains the comments by Sawaki, an eminent modern Sōtō priest, on the waka collection, and vol. 17 contains his comments on the Chinese collection, especially Menzan's version). For a broader and fuller discussion of Dōgen's impact on Ryōkan and the ideological relation between their respective bodies of work, see Nakamura Sōichi, *Ryōkan no ge to Shōbōgenzō* (Tokyo: Seishin shobō, 1984); Nakamura also

wrote a modern translation and commentary on the *Shōbōgenzō*.

2. This poem is cited in Kagamishima Genryū, ed., *Dōgen zenji goroku* (Tokyo: Kodansha, 1990), pp. 5–6. A translation of the entire poem appears in *Moon in a Dewdrop: Writings of Zen Master Dōgen,* Kazuaki Tanahashi, ed. (San Francisco: North Point Press, 1985), pp. 223–34. Notice how the next to last line refers to "after a while," which is a typical part of the structure of the *Eihei kōroku* sermons.